The Homemade
Ice Cream
Book

The Homemade
Ice Cream
Book

BERNICE HURST

A QUINTET BOOK

Published by New Burlington Books,
6 Blundell Street,
London N7

ISBN 0 948872 03 9

Reprinted 1989

This book was designed and produced by
Quintet Publishing Limited
6 Blundell Street, London N7

Art Director Peter Bridgewater
Editor Suzanne Luchford
Photographer David Gallant
Home Economist and Styling Sara Beaugeard
assisted by Pene Sydenham
Illustrator Annie Ellis

Photographs on pages 27, 41, 60, 63, 83, 88, 91, 92,
93, 108, 111, 124, and 127
© Quintet Publishing Limited

Typeset in Great Britain by
Central Southern Typesetting, Eastbourne
Manufactured in Hong Kong by Regent Publishing
Services Ltd
Printed in Hong Kong by Leefung-Asco Printers
Limited

The author and publishers are grateful to Covent
Garden Kitchen Supplies, David Mellor and
Divertimenti of London, ICTC of Isleworth and
Loose's of Norwich for supplying equipment for
photography; Baskin-Robbins International
Company of London and Birds Eye Wall's Limited
of Walton-on-Thames for permission to reproduce
selected photographs.

◆ CONTENTS ◆

Introduction

HOMEMADE ICE CREAM is a luxury dessert for all occasions. Ice creams are fun, they are simple and easy to make with their delightful texture and luscious flavours. They have advantages over other desserts as they can be prepared well in advance and the flavouring possibilities are infinite. This book introduces you to the art of creative ice cream making, providing recipes and giving ideas for experimentation with a whole host of subtle tastes from liqueurs, herbs and spices to nuts and exotic fruits from around the world. You can have endless fun mixing and matching tantalizing flavours with textures, tastes and accompaniments.

At one time, bought ice creams were of poor quality with an extremely limited choice of flavours, but these days with the advent of supermarkets, refrigeration and home freezers and with an immense choice of commercially prepared flavours why should anyone make ice cream at home? Surely it is more economical and far less time-consuming to purchase a selection of flavours than to seek out ingredients and spend time whisking, stirring, blending and freezing? The answer lies in the current attitude to food – that it should be natural. Homemade ice cream uses fresh ingredients and, unlike the commercial product, there is no loss of flavour as a result of storing it in a freezer for an unspecified length of time. The preparation can be as enjoyable as the consumption, and what better reason can there be for making your own ice cream than that? It only takes a little effort to achieve that pleasure. Use the recipes to start you on your way.

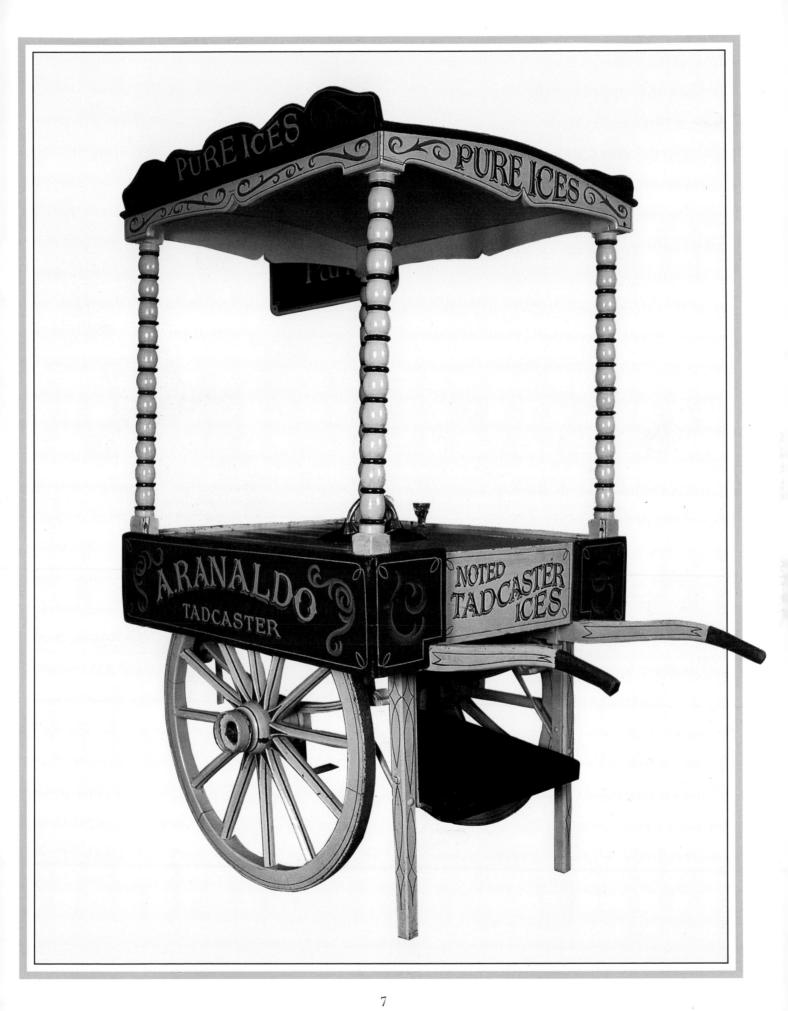

◆ *ICE CREAM MAKERS* ◆

UNLESS you are setting up home for the first time, you will probably have most of the items needed for ice cream making in your kitchen already. Few of them are inflexible – you can always find a substitute. For example, a small glass placed upside down in a cake pan can replace that ring pan you haven't got. It is a good idea to save empty plastic boxes and cartons of all shapes and sizes for storing ice cream.

◆ *EQUIPMENT* ◆

ICE CREAM makers are not essential equipment. They do, however, make superb ice cream, often in a very short time. They vary a great deal, from one manufacturer to another, in terms of the amount of effort one has to put in, their ease of cleaning, the noise they make, and the space they require. All this, plus their range in price and the frequency with which they will be used, must be taken into account before deciding whether or not, and which kind, to purchase.

Early ice creams were made in containers surrounded by ice and salt. They needed constant stirring. Later churn freezers simplified matters slightly – ice and salt were still necessary but the container had a handle which was attached to a paddle inside the freezing container. You (or the maid or children) simply had to turn the handle until the ice cream froze.

Today we have a wider choice. Electric sorbetières with their own motors for refrigeration, or models which still need ice but will churn the mixture automatically, are available. Alternatively, there are machines which are placed directly in the freezer. These are operated by a lead (wire) which extends from the freezer to the nearest plug so that the ice cream is churned constantly. Many machines produce ice cream which is still soft, so if you would like it to be firm enough to scoop, it must be transferred to a mould (mold) or container and frozen directly in the freezer.

To ensure a perfectly smooth ice cream, if you do not have a sorbetière, the ice crystals should be stirred from the outer edge into the centre of the mixture occasionally during freezing. When it is at

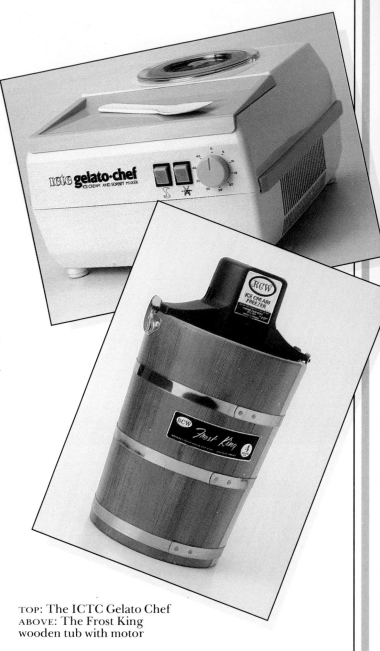

TOP: The ICTC Gelato Chef
ABOVE: The Frost King
wooden tub with motor

the half frozen stage, transfer the ice cream to a bowl, and whisk the mixture to make it light and even textured. This does mean being available for as long as it takes for the ice cream to freeze, but it is a worthwhile occupation. Otherwise, choose a parfait or mousse that does not need stirring.

ulds (molds)

hand whisk

freezing trays

shallow
freezing tray

shallow
mould (mold)

flat baking
(cookie) sheet

square cake pan

lemon zester
(rinder)
(cannelle knife)

fluted
mould (mold)

fancy detachable
mould (mold)

loaf pan

Ice Cream

REFRIGERATION popularized ice cream. Before regular deliveries of ice – and the means to store it – became possible, only royalty and the aristocracy were able to enjoy ice cream. But, with the invention of ice boxes, refrigerators and freezers, both portable and domestic, ice cream became a snack. It became customary to end an afternoon or evening stroll with an ice cream. Street corner vendors sold paper cups and later waffles and cones filled with ice cream. Café society spooned coupes and sundaes. Teenagers went out for 'malts' and 'sodas'. Mobile vans and bikes rang their bells all over town.

The quest for new taste sensations began – who could create the most intriguing, sensational and delicious ice cream of all? The Café Procope in Paris was serving as many as 80 varieties as early as 1782. Baskin Robbins, an American ice cream manufacturer, has an entry in *The Guinness Book of Records* for developing over 400 different kinds of ice cream. Cookbooks and food magazines abound with 'new' recipes.

Ice cream today is a cult. Exponents of Nouvelle Cuisine vie to create light, refreshing sorbets. Gourmets the world over try to find new combinations of flavours and sorbetières are often given pride of place in the kitchen. As there is an increasing trend towards pure natural ingredients and the labels of commercial products are read avidly, imagination at home reigns supreme. Refrigeration has introduced us to exotic ingredients grown in countries (or regions) other than our own. It has also given us access to out of season ingredients. Both domestic and commercial ice cream making is at its peak – there is no reason why a snack cannot be a luxury.

But, on a more practical note, a couple of hints may help before you embark on making your own ice cream. First, taste while mixing – the mixture should be a little bit stronger or sweeter than you would like as flavour diminishes during freezing. Next, use a shallow tray for speed in freezing and defrosting. When a recipe includes alcohol the ice cream will take longer to freeze. Soften the ice cream in the refrigerator before serving – if you leave it at room temperature, the outside will get soft while the inside remains hard. Ice cream needs to be firm for scooping but remember that soft ice cream can be piped to create a visual effect when serving. Smaller portions should be served as homemade ice cream is generally far richer than commercially available varieties.

◆ *CUSTARD ICE CREAM* ◆

◇ *INGREDIENTS* ◇

SERVES 8

4 eggs

½ cup/125 g/4 oz sugar

2 cups/450 ml/16 fl oz single (light) cream

5 ml sp/1 tsp vanilla essence (extract)

1 cup/225 ml/8 fl oz whipping cream

◇ *PREPARATION* ◇

◇ Beat the eggs with the sugar until the mixture is very thick and light. Scald the single (light) cream with the vanilla. Pour over the eggs and mix well.

◇ Transfer the custard to the top of a double boiler and heat, stirring constantly, until it is thick enough to coat the back of the spoon. Leave to cool.

◇ Whisk the whipping cream until it is just beginning to thicken. Fold carefully into the cooled custard, starting with just one spoonful and gradually adding the remainder.

◇ If you are flavouring the ice cream, add your other ingredients at this stage.

◇ Pour the custard into a shallow freezer tray or plastic box. Cover and freeze for 1–2 hours. Turn into a large bowl and mix well so that all the particles of ice which have formed are thoroughly mixed in. Return to the freezer. You can now leave the ice cream until it is firm, or repeat the mixing procedure. The more you mix, the smoother the finished ice cream will be.

◇ Transfer the ice cream to the refrigerator for 30 minutes before serving.

VARIATION For a lighter custard, substitute milk for single (light) cream and omit the whipping cream.

For a classic vanilla ice cream, substitute a split vanilla pod for the vanilla essence (extract) when scalding the cream. Remove the pod before pouring the cream over the egg yolks, but split it open and scrape the seeds into the custard. Alternatively, 2 tbsp/25 g/1 oz coffee beans or ½ cup/125 g/4 oz grated dark chocolate can be heated with the cream.

◆ *PARFAIT ICE CREAM* ◆

◇ I N G R E D I E N T S ◇

SERVES 8

¾ cup/175 g/6 oz sugar

60 ml/4 tbsp water

4 egg yolks

1½ cups/350 ml/12 fl oz double (heavy) cream

◇ P R E P A R A T I O N ◇

◇ Heat the sugar in the water over a medium heat until it has dissolved.

◇ Raise the heat and boil the syrup for 30 seconds.

◇ Whisk the egg yolks until they are very thick and light.

◇ Pour the hot syrup over the yolks, whisking constantly. Continue whisking until the mixture has cooled down and thickened. To speed this process up, you can place the mixing bowl in a bowl of ice.

◇ If you are flavouring the ice cream, add the remaining ingredients at this stage.

◇ Whisk the cream until it is thick. Fold into the egg mixture, starting with just one spoonful and gradually adding the remainder.

◇ A stiffly beaten egg white can also be folded in if you would like the parfait to be somewhat lighter.

◇ Parfait ice creams do not need to be stirred while freezing. This makes them particularly suitable for moulding (molding) into interesting shapes. Pour the mixture into a tray, box, cake pan or mould (mold), cover and freeze until firm.

◇ If you are going to unmould (unmold) the ice cream, run a warm cloth over the surface and turn out onto an attractive serving dish. Decorate with nuts, crushed macaroons, cream or fruit and leave in the refrigerator for 15 minutes before serving. If you want to prepare the parfait in advance, turn out the mould (mold), decorate and return to the freezer until 15 minutes before serving.

◆ *EXTRA CREAM ICE CREAM* ◆

◇ *INGREDIENTS* ◇
SERVES 8
4 eggs
2½ ml/½ tsp vanilla essence (extract)
½ cup/125 g/4 oz sugar
1¼ cups/300 ml/10 fl oz double (heavy) cream

EXTRA CREAM ICE CREAM

◇ PREPARATION ◇

1 Separate the eggs.

2 Add the sugar and vanilla to the egg yolks.

3 Whisk the yolk mixture until very thick and pale.

4 Whisk the cream until it is just thick enough to hold its shape.

5 Carefully fold the cream into the yolk mixture, starting with just one spoonful and gradually adding the remainder.

If you are flavouring the ice cream, add the remaining ingredients at this stage.

6 Whisk the egg whites until they are stiff but not dry.

7 Carefully fold into the cream mixture, starting with just one spoonful and gradually adding the remainder.

8 Pour into a shallow freezer tray or plastic box. Cover and freeze for 1–2 hours. Turn into a large bowl and mix well so that all the particles of ice which have formed are thoroughly mixed in. Return to the freezer. You can now leave the ice cream until it is firm, or repeat the mixing procedure. The more you mix, the smoother the finished ice cream will be.

Transfer the ice cream to the refrigerator for 30 minutes before serving.

◆ EASY ICE CREAM ◆

◇ INGREDIENTS ◇

SERVES 8

2½ cups/575 ml/1 pt double (heavy) cream

½ cup/125 g/4 oz sugar

◇ PREPARATION ◇

◇ Whisk the cream until it is just thick enough to hold its shape. Fold in the sugar and any flavouring you have decided to use. Pour into a shallow freezer tray or plastic box, cover and freeze for 1–2 hours. Whisk well and return to the freezer until firm. For those with a particularly sweet tooth, use sieved (sifted) icing (confectioners') sugar.

◇ This is the easiest ice cream to flavour — simply stir in chopped or puréed fresh, dried or glacé fruit, nuts, chocolate or candy. Alternatively, use this recipe as a base for a rippled ice cream. After stirring the half frozen cream, gently swirl in a purée of chocolate, chestnuts or fruit.

◆ EXTRA LIGHT ICE CREAM ◆

◇ I N G R E D I E N T S ◇

SERVES 8

1 cup/250 g/8 oz sugar

1¼ cups/300 ml/10 fl oz water

4 egg whites

1¼ cups/300 ml/10 fl oz whipping cream

◇ P R E P A R A T I O N ◇

◇ Stir the sugar in the water over a medium heat until it has dissolved. Boil rapidly for 5 minutes.

◇ Whisk the egg whites until they are stiff but not dry. Slowly pour in the hot syrup, whisking constantly. Continue beating until the whites are very thick and light and the mixture has completely cooled. This step can be speeded up by placing the bowl in a bowl full of ice cubes.

◇ Beat the cream until it is just thick enough to hold its shape. Carefully fold into the egg whites, starting with just one spoonful and gradually adding the remainder.

◇ If you are flavouring the ice cream, very gently add the remaining ingredients at this stage.

◇ Pour the ice cream into a freezer tray, plastic box, bowl or mould (mold). Cover and freeze until firm. This ice cream is particularly suitable for shaping and unmoulding (unmolding) as it does not need to be stirred while it is freezing.

◇ If you are going to unmould (unmold) the ice cream, run a warm cloth over the surface and turn out onto an attractive serving dish. Decorate with nuts, crushed macaroons, cream or fruit and leave in the refrigerator for 15 minutes before serving. If you want to prepare the parfait in advance, turn out the mould (mold), decorate and return to the freezer until 15 minutes before serving.

◆ FLAVOUR VARIATIONS ◆

The following flavouring ideas can be added to any of the basic ice creams on pages 14–19.

Praline made from ½ cup/125 g/4 oz sugar, and almonds, if ground: 1 cup/125 g/4 oz; if whole: ¾ cup/125 g/4 oz or peanut/walnut brittle made in the same way. Chop or crush according to how chunky you like your ice cream.

Hazelnuts (filberts), pecans or almonds, crushed or chopped. Try toasting the nuts in the oven first or tossing them in melted butter until golden.

Chopped pistachio nuts.

Toasted coconut.

Unsweetened chestnut purée.

Crumbled cake, meringues, macaroons, wafers or biscuits (cookies).

Broken sweets (candy) — mints, chocolates, diced marshmallows.

Diced fresh, brandied or glacé (candied) fruit (soaked in spirit if you like).

Puréed fresh fruit or poached dried fruit. Use syrup, apple juice or white wine to enliven a fresh fruit purée or cook the dried fruit. If you like contrasting textures, mash or chop the fruit coarsely.

Diced crystallized (candied) fruit peel.

Mincemeat, especially with extra rum or brandy.

Any alcohol, wine or liqueur you like, especially combined with fruit.

Honey can be added to ice cream instead of sugar.

Stir in a few drops of orange or rose flower water, especially with plain, fruit or nut ice cream.

For custard ice creams, add poppy seeds, strong tea or coffee when the milk is heating.

To make rippled ice cream, wait until the mixture is half frozen and has been stirred once or twice. Spoon a thick purée of fruit, chocolate, coffee or chestnuts over the top and gently swirl with a knife. Peanut butter (smooth or crunchy) is a delicious alternative.

◇ If you already have some ice cream in the freezer and want to dress it up, transfer to the refrigerator until it is just beginning to soften and add the flavouring of your choice or use it as a base for a rippled ice cream.

❖ *CHOCOLATE ICE CREAM* ❖

◇ PREPARATION ◇

◇ Break the chocolate into small pieces and heat with the milk, stirring constantly, until the chocolate has melted and the milk is just about to boil. Either milk or plain (light or dark) chocolate can be used.

◇ Whisk the egg or yolks with the sugar until very thick and light.

◇ Pour the milk over the eggs, whisking constantly. Transfer to the top of a double boiler and heat, still stirring, until the custard is thick enough to coat the back of the spoon. Leave to cool.

◇ Whisk the cream until it is just beginning to thicken. Carefully fold into the custard. If you are adding any other flavourings, gently stir them in at this stage.

◇ Pour the ice cream mixture into a freezer tray or plastic box, cover and freeze for 1–2 hours. Whisk well so that all the ice crystals are mixed in and the ice cream is smooth. Return to the freezer until firm.

VARIATION Chocolate can be combined and enhanced by a whole host of ingredients — so many that they cannot all be listed here. Try adding any of the following or creating your own combinations!

Chopped or ground hazelnuts (filberts) or chopped or ground almonds and a few drops of almond essence (extract).

Crushed or chopped praline.

Raisins soaked in dark rum.

Chocolate drops or diced chocolate mints and a few drops of peppermint essence (extract).

Diced marshmallows.

Unsweetened chestnut purée and diced marron glacé (plus a spoonful of alcohol for a party effect — try sherry, brandy or Kirsch).

Diced glacé (candied) cherries or maraschino cherries (and a splash of liqueur for that extra something).

Almost any spirit, for example rum, Cointreau, brandy, Kahlua, which may also be enhanced by pieces of diced fruit like oranges or cherries.

A few spoonfuls of strong black coffee with Tia Maria, Kahlua or Crème de Cacao.

Broken biscuits (cookies), for example meringues, wafers, ginger nuts (ginger snaps).

◇ INGREDIENTS ◇

SERVES 6

½ cup/125 g/4 oz chocolate
1 cup/225 ml/8 fl oz milk
1 egg or 2 egg yolks
¼ cup/50 g/2 oz sugar
1 cup/225 ml/8 fl oz double (heavy) cream

◆ CARAMEL ICE CREAM ◆

◇ I N G R E D I E N T S ◇

SERVES 4

60 ml/4 tbsp sugar

75 ml/6 tbsp water

2 egg yolks

1¼ cups/300 ml/10 fl oz double (heavy) cream

◇ P R E P A R A T I O N ◇

◇ Place the sugar and a third of the water in a heavy-based pan. Stir over a medium heat until the sugar has dissolved. Raise the heat, boil rapidly until brown in colour and add the remaining water.

◇ Whisk the egg yolks until they are thick and light. Slowly pour on the hot caramel and continue whisking until the mixture is thick and cold.

◇ Whisk the cream until it is just beginning to thicken. Carefully fold into the eggs and caramel.

◇ Pour the ice cream mixture into a freezer tray or plastic box, cover and freeze for 1–2 hours. Whisk well and return to the freezer until firm.

APRICOT ICE CREAM

◇ INGREDIENTS ◇

SERVES 6

½ cup/125 g/4 oz dried apricots

½ cup/125 ml/4 fl oz dry white wine

½ cup/125 g/4 oz sugar

⅔ cup/150 ml/5 fl oz water

2 egg whites

⅔ cup/150 ml/5 fl oz whipping cream

few drops almond essence (extract) (optional)

◇ PREPARATION ◇

◇ Dice the apricots and cook in an uncovered pan with the white wine for 15–20 minutes or until they are soft. If the liquid evaporates, add some apple juice. Cool the apricots and then sieve or liquidize them to make a smooth purée. If you have less than ⅔ cup/150 ml/5 oz when you are finished, make up to that quantity with unsweetened apple juice.

◇ Stir the sugar into the water over a medium heat until it has dissolved. Boil rapidly for 5 minutes.

◇ Whisk the egg whites until they are stiff but not dry. Slowly pour in the hot syrup, whisking constantly. Beat until the meringue is very thick.

◇ Whisk the cream until it is just beginning to thicken. Carefully fold the fruit purée into the egg whites and then add the whipped cream, starting with one spoonful and gradually adding the remainder. Stir in the almond essence (extract).

◇ Turn the ice cream mixture into a loaf pan, ring mould (mold) or cake pan. Cover and freeze until firm. This ice cream does not need to be stirred while freezing. Unmould (unmold) and serve garnished with slices of fresh or tinned apricots or a puréed sauce made from fresh fruit or poached dried fruit. Toasted almonds can also be sprinkled on top.

VARIATION Replace the dried apricots with fresh (skinned), bottled or tinned (canned) apricots. Drain well, purée and add 15 ml/1 tbsp white wine.

Other fruits can be used according to availability with equal success. Firm fruit such as plums, greengages (small green plums) or pears should be cooked in syrup, apple juice or wine if they are fresh. Dried fruit such as prunes need to be poached. Soft fruits such as strawberries, or pineapple need only be liquidized and sieved before adding to the egg whites.

◆ STRAWBERRY ICE CREAM ◆

◇ INGREDIENTS ◇

SERVES 6

½ cup/125 g/4 oz sugar

1¼ cups/300 ml/10 fl oz water

1⅓ cups/250 g/8 oz strawberries

1¼ cups/300 ml/10 fl oz double (heavy) cream

2 egg whites (optional)

◇ PREPARATION ◇

◇ Heat the sugar in the water, stirring constantly over a medium heat, until it has dissolved. Boil rapidly for 5 minutes then leave until cold.

◇ Sieve or liquidize the strawberries and then mix them with the cold syrup.

◇ Whisk the cream until it is just beginning to thicken. Gently fold the cream into the fruit purée.

◇ Whisk the egg whites, if used, until they are stiff but not dry. Fold into the fruit mixture.

◇ Turn into a freezer tray or plastic box, cover and freeze for 1–2 hours.

◇ Whisk until all the ice crystals have been well mixed in. Return to the freezer until firm.

VARIATION Sieve or liquidize the strawberries with icing (confectioners') sugar instead of a sugar syrup. Mix with cream and egg whites as above. Any soft summer berry, such as blackberries, raspberries, redcurrants, can be used in the same way. Firmer berries, such as gooseberries or blackcurrants, should be cooked on a very low heat with the sugar before being puréed. Other summer fruit, such as peaches, apricots or plums, should be skinned by plunging them into boiling water for a minute or two and then cooked in a sugar syrup, apple juice or white wine before liquidizing. The purée can then be used as above. If you are using a sugar syrup to make the ice cream, the general rule is to use equal amounts of syrup and fruit purée. One or more spoonfuls of lemon juice can also be added to sharpen the taste of the fruit and counteract the heaviness of the sugar and cream combination.

◆ PINEAPPLE ICE CREAM ◆

◇ I N G R E D I E N T S ◇

SERVES 8

¾ cup/175 g/6 oz sugar

2 cups/450 ml/16 fl oz water

1 lemon

2 cups/450 g/1 lb crushed, fresh pineapple

1¼ cups/300 ml/10 fl oz double (heavy) cream

2 egg whites (optional)

◇ P R E P A R A T I O N ◇

◇ Stir the sugar in the water over a medium heat until it has dissolved. Add the finely grated lemon rind and boil rapidly for 5 minutes. Leave until thoroughly cooled.

◇ Combine the crushed pineapple and lemon juice. Measure and mix with an equal amount of syrup.

◇ Whisk the cream until it is just beginning to thicken. Carefully fold into the fruit purée.

◇ Whisk the egg whites until they are stiff but not dry. Gently fold into the fruit.

◇ Pour the ice cream mixture into a freezer tray or plastic box, cover and freeze for 1–2 hours. Whisk well so that all the ice crystals are mixed in. Return to the freezer until firm.

◇ Note: tinned (canned) pineapple can be used very successfully for this ice cream. If you are using fresh pineapple, save the shell and pile the ice cream into it before serving.

◆ TANGERINE ICE CREAM ◆

◇ INGREDIENTS ◇

SERVES 6

¾ cup/175 g/6 oz sugar

1¼ cups/300 ml/10 fl oz water

8 tangerines

½ lemon

1¼ cups/300 ml/10 fl oz double (heavy) cream

◇ PREPARATION ◇

◇ Stir the sugar in the water over a medium heat until it has dissolved. Add the finely grated lemon rind and boil rapidly for 5 minutes. Leave until thoroughly cooled.

◇ Cut a slice off the top of each tangerine and very carefully cut out the fruit pulp. Save the tops. Be sure not to damage the tangerine skins or cut through to the bottom as the shell will be filled with ice cream for serving. Set 6 of the shells aside. Finely grate the rind of the remaining shells and reserve.

◇ Squeeze the fruit pulp to extract as much juice as possible. Combine 1¼ cups/300 ml/10 fl oz of the tangerine juice with the lemon juice, syrup and grated rind.

◇ Pour the fruit juice into a freezer tray or plastic box, cover and freeze until it is mushy. Whisk well until it is smooth.

◇ Whisk the cream until it is just beginning to thicken. Carefully fold into the partially frozen fruit juice. Return to the freezer for 1–2 hours, whisk again and freeze until firm.

◇ Fill the reserved tangerine shells with ice cream, brush the outside with water so that they will set and return to the freezer until 15 minutes before serving. Replace the top of each tangerine, using them as natural fruit lids.

VARIATION Oranges, lemons, limes or grapefruit can be substituted for tangerines. Be sure to use equal quantities of fruit juice and sugar syrup for the fruit ice. If you are using lemons or limes, only half the quantity of cream will be needed.

◈ MAPLE WALNUT ICE CREAM ◈

◇ INGREDIENTS ◇

SERVES 8

⅔ cup/150 ml/5 fl oz maple syrup

4 egg yolks

1¼ cups/300 ml/10 fl oz double (heavy) cream

½ cup/125 g/4 oz chopped walnuts

◇ PREPARATION ◇

◇ Boil the maple syrup until it is very thick.

◇ Beat the egg yolks until they are very thick and light. Pour into the top of a double boiler and slowly add the hot syrup, whisking constantly. Continue beating the yolks and syrup in the double boiler until it thickens to the consistency of whipped cream. Remove the top of the double boiler from the heat and stand in a bowl full of ice cubes. Continue beating the yolks until they are completely cold.

◇ Whisk the cream until it is thick enough to hold its shape. Carefully fold into the yolk mixture, starting with just one spoonful and gradually adding the remainder. Stir in the walnuts.

◇ Pour the ice cream mixture into a plastic tray or mould (mold), cover and freeze. This ice cream does not need stirring (see Parfait Ice Cream page 15) while it is freezing and one can therefore unmould (unmold) it, as described on page 15. Serve in slices or scoops, decorated with glazed walnut halves and a rum, brandy or coffee sauce.

◆ *GINGER ICE CREAM* ◆

◇ *INGREDIENTS* ◇

SERVES 6

3 egg yolks

¼ cup/50 g/2 oz sugar

½ cup/125 g/4 oz stem ginger

15 ml/1 tbsp ginger syrup

1¼ cups/300 ml/10 fl oz milk

⅔ cup/150 ml/5 fl oz double (heavy) cream

◇ *PREPARATION* ◇

◇ Whisk the egg yolks with the sugar until very light and thick.

◇ Drain and dice the stem ginger. Stir into the eggs along with the ginger syrup.

◇ Scald the milk and slowly pour over the eggs, whisking constantly. Pour the custard into the top of a double boiler and heat, stirring constantly, until it is thick enough to coat the back of the spoon. Leave to cool.

◇ Pour the custard into a freezer tray or plastic box, cover and freeze for 1–2 hours. Transfer to a bowl and whisk until it is smooth and all the ice crystals have been mixed in.

◇ Whisk the cream until it is just beginning to thicken. Gently fold into the custard. Pour into the freezer tray again, cover and freeze until firm.

VARIATION Omit the stem ginger and flavour the custard with 2½ ml/1 tsp ground ginger or 15 ml/ 1 tbsp grated fresh ginger and 15 ml/1 tbsp crystallized (candied) ginger pieces.

Following the method described above, a liqueur may be added to the custard mixture. For extra variation, omit the ginger and divide the custard into separate containers and add a different liqueur — Benedictine, Crème de Menthe, Kahlua, Tia Maria, Cassis — to each batch. Serve a tiny scoop of each kind in either glass dishes, or as a filling for miniature meringues, or in a pie shell made from biscuit (cookie) crumbs in *tulipes* (see page 112). Alternatively, freeze the flavours in small sandwich pans and assemble a multi-coloured gâteau.

◆ GLACÉ (CANDIED) FRUIT ◆
ICE CREAM

◇ *INGREDIENTS* ◇

SERVES 4

15 ml/1 tbsp raisins

15 ml/1 tbsp dark rum

¾ cup/175 ml/6 fl oz double (heavy) cream

⅓ cup/40 g/1½ oz icing (confectioners') sugar

2½ ml/½ tsp vanilla essence (extract)

15 ml/1 tbsp glacé (candied) cherries

15 ml/1 tbsp angelica or mixed peel

2 egg whites

◇ *PREPARATION* ◇

◇ Soak the raisins in the rum overnight.
◇ Whisk the cream until it is just beginning to thicken. Carefully fold in the sieved (sifted) sugar and add the vanilla essence (extract).

◇ Dice the cherries, angelica or mixed peel and the raisins. Stir into the cream.
◇ Whisk the egg whites until they are stiff but not dry. Gently fold into the cream, starting with just one spoonful and gradually adding the remainder.
◇ Pour the ice cream mixture into a freezer tray or plastic box, cover and freeze for 1–2 hours. Beat well so that all the ice crystals are mixed in and return to the freezer until firm. For a particularly smooth ice cream, repeat the mixing procedure once or twice more.

VARIATION Substitute fruit which has been preserved in alcohol (see page 119) for all or part of the glacé (candied) fruit. Other dried fruits can replace the raisins — try figs or prunes soaked in brandy or apricots in white wine. Omit the cherries and angelica but add praline or glazed walnuts either in the ice cream or as a garnish when serving.

◆ CREAMY YOGURT ICE CREAM ◆

◇ INGREDIENTS ◇

SERVES 8

⅓ cup/75 g/3 oz sugar

1 cup/225 ml/8 fl oz blackcurrant purée

15 ml/1 tbsp Cassis (optional)

¾ cup/175 ml/6 fl oz unsweetened yogurt

⅔ cup/150 ml/5 fl oz double (heavy) cream

◇ PREPARATION ◇

◇ Stir the sugar into the blackcurrant purée until it has dissolved. Add the Cassis, if used, and yogurt. Mix well.

◇ Whisk the cream until it is just beginning to thicken. Fold into the fruit purée.

◇ Pour into a freezer tray or plastic box, cover and freeze, stirring once when it is mushy.

VARIATION Substitute peach or raspberry purée flavoured with Kirsch, orange or lemon juice mixed with white wine, cooked apples or pears mixed with cider, strawberries flavoured with lime juice, Grand Marnier or any other combination that sounds tempting.

For a crunchy ice cream, stir a few spoonfuls of muesli (or granola) or toasted oatmeal into the yogurt. Dried fruit soaked in apple juice or spirit can also be added. The simplest yogurt ice cream can be made by mixing chunks of fruit, or a purée with the yogurt and freezing as instructed above. A lightly whisked egg white can also be folded in to make the ice cream lighter.

This recipe is also superb with purées of exotic fruit such as mango, passion fruit, or papaya. The fruit should be sweetened, according to taste, and used instead of the blackcurrant purée in the recipe above.

◆ CHERRY YOGURT ICE CREAM ◆

◇ INGREDIENTS ◇

SERVES 6

¾ cup/175 g/6 oz sugar

30 ml/2 tbsp lemon juice

⅔ cup/150 ml/5 fl oz water

1½ cups/350 g/12 oz cherries [stoned (pitted) weight]

2 eggs

1¼ cups/300 ml/10 oz natural yogurt

15 ml/1 tbsp cherry brandy or liqueur (optional)

◇ PREPARATION ◇

◇ Stir the sugar in the combined water and lemon juice over a medium heat until it has dissolved. Boil rapidly for 5 minutes. Reduce the heat, add the stoned (pitted) cherries and cook gently until the cherries are soft. Drain the cherries and set aside. If you prefer, bottled or tinned (canned) cherries can be used.

◇ Beat the yolks until they are thick and light. Slowly pour in the syrup, whisking constantly. Continue beating until the yolks are thick again and completely cooled.

◇ Lightly whisk the yogurt so that it is smooth. Carefully fold into the yolks, starting with just one spoonful and gradually adding the remainder.

◇ Stir in the cherries and brandy or liqueur.

◇ Pour the mixture into a freezer tray or plastic box, cover and freeze for 1–2 hours. Return to the mixing bowl and whisk until smooth.

◇ Beat the egg whites until they are stiff but not dry. Gently fold into the ice cream. Pour back into the freezer tray or plastic box, cover and freeze until firm.

◇ For a special occasion, serve the ice cream with flambéed cherries.

VARIATION Replace the cherries with any other berry or soft fruit and replace the cherry brandy with a spirit of a complimentary flavour, for example blackcurrants and Cassis, raspberries and Kirsch, plums and gin, bananas and rum.

◆ BANANA AND HONEY ◆ ICE CREAM

◇ INGREDIENTS ◇

SERVES 4

¾ cup/175 g/6 oz mashed bananas

30 ml/2 tbsp honey

15 ml/1 tbsp lemon juice

⅔ cup/150 ml/5 oz natural yogurt

1 egg white

◇ PREPARATION ◇

◇ Mash or liquidize the bananas until they are smooth. Blend in the honey, lemon juice and yogurt.

◇ Pour the mixture into a freezer tray or plastic box, cover and freeze for 1–2 hours. Beat very well to remove all the ice crystals.

◇ Whisk the egg white until it is stiff but not dry. Carefully fold into the banana mixture, starting with just one spoonful and gradually adding the remainder. Spoon into the freezer tray or box, cover and return to the freezer until the ice cream is firm.

◆ *AVOCADO ICE CREAM* ◆

◇ *INGREDIENTS* ◇

SERVES 4

1 avocado

15 ml/1 tbsp lime juice

30 ml/2 tbsp single (cereal or light) cream

1 egg white

◇ *PREPARATION* ◇

◇ Peel the avocado, cut in half and remove the stone. Mash or purée it until it is smooth. Stir in the lime juice and cream, beating well to ensure that the mixture is well blended and completely smooth.

◇ Whisk the egg white until it is stiff but not dry. Gently fold into the avocado mixture, starting with just one spoonful and gradually adding the remainder.

◇ Pour into a freezer tray or plastic box, cover and freeze for 1–2 hours.

◇ Beat well so that all the ice crystals are mixed in. Return to the freezer until firm.

◆ BROWN BREAD ICE CREAM ◆

◇ INGREDIENTS ◇

SERVES 4

5 ml/1 tsp oil

1 cup/50 g/2 oz wholemeal (whole wheat) bread crumbs

¼ cup/50 g/2 oz brown sugar

1¼ cups/300 ml/10 fl oz whipping cream

30 ml/2 tbsp sugar

2½ ml/½ tsp vanilla essence (extract) (optional)

◇ PREPARATION ◇

◇ Brush the oil over the surface of a flat baking tray or Swiss roll (jelly roll) pan. Sprinkle on the crumbs and sugar. Place under a hot grill (broiler) and cook, stirring frequently, until the sugar has melted and the crumbs are well toasted. Leave to cool and then crumble again if the mixture has solidified.

◇ Beat the cream with the sugar until it is stiff and add the optional vanilla essence (extract) at this point.

◇ Fold the crumbs into the cream. Turn the mixture into a freezer tray, cover and freeze for 1–2 hours. Beat well and return to the freezer until firm.

◇ Serve with a hot coffee or butterscotch sauce (see pages 125 and 126) and, for a special occasion, spoon some brandied figs on top.

VARIATION Substitute oatmeal for the bread crumbs. Diced or puréed prunes (soaked and cooked) blend especially well with the oats.

◆ MANGO ICE CREAM ◆ PUMPKIN PIE ICE CREAM ◆

◇ INGREDIENTS ◇
SERVES 6
½ quantity custard ice cream recipe (see page 14)
450 g/1 lb mango
¼ cup/50 g/2 oz sugar
1 lime

◇ PREPARATION ◇

◇ Make the custard ice cream as instructed and leave to cool.

◇ Peel the mango, remove the stone and purée the flesh with the sugar and lime juice.

◇ If you are using tinned (canned) or bottled fruit, drain well before using.

◇ Fold the fruit into the custard. Turn into a freezer tray or plastic box and freeze as instructed.

VARIATION Any other exotic fruit can be puréed and mixed into custard ice cream in the same way — passion fruit, pineapple, kiwi fruit are delicious.

◇ INGREDIENTS ◇
SERVES 6
½ quantity custard ice cream recipe (see page 14)
2 cups/1 lb/450 g cooked pumpkin
½ cup/125 g/4 oz sugar
2½ ml/½ tsp each ground cloves, ground ginger, ground nutmeg, mixed spice and salt
15 ml/1 tbsp brandy (optional)

◇ PREPARATION ◇

◇ Make the custard ice cream as instructed and leave to cool.

◇ Mash or purée the pumpkin until it is smooth.

◇ Combine the sugar and spices. Beat into the pumpkin purée. Stir in the brandy if you are using it.

◇ Fold the pumpkin purée into the custard. Turn into a freezer tray or plastic box and freeze as instructed. Serve the ice cream garnished with chopped, glazed walnuts or pecans and either butterscotch or marshmallow sauce (see page 126).

◆ CHRISTMAS PUDDING ◆
ICE CREAM

◇ INGREDIENTS ◇

SERVES 8

1 quantity extra cream ice cream recipe (see page 16)

½ cup/125 g/4 oz unsweetened chestnut purée

30 ml/2 tbsp plain (semi-sweet) chocolate drops

30 ml/2 tbsp marron glacé, diced

30 ml/2 tbsp brandied fruit (see page 119), diced

◇ PREPARATION ◇

◇ Make the ice cream as instructed, beating in the chestnut purée just before adding the whipped cream. Fold in the chocolate drops, diced marron glacé and fruit after the cream. Fold in the egg whites and freeze as instructed.

◇ The brandied fruit can either be fresh fruit which has been preserved in alcohol (for example mandarins, cherries, raspberries) or dried fruit which is soaked in brandy for 2 hours before being used for the ice cream. Dice the fruit into small pieces before adding to the ice cream. The alcohol need not necessarily be brandy — raisins may be soaked in rum and dried apricots poached in white wine and cooled work equally well. If you are good at planning ahead, cherries can be bottled in gin during the summer then left until Christmas to provide a luscious fruit, already tainted with alcohol, for ice cream desserts. There is really no ironclad recipe for this ice cream. Crushed macaroons, brandy snaps or ginger nuts (ginger snaps) can also be added, as can preserved ginger, crushed praline or a few spoonfuls of your favourite mincemeat. The ice cream itself can also be flavoured with sherry, Marsala or any other spirit, according to preference.

VARIATION If you have some ice cream already made in the freezer, transfer it to the refrigerator until it is slightly soft. Beat in any of the above ingredients and re-freeze, whisking it just once to prevent the formation of ice crystals.

Christmas Pudding Ice Cream can also be softened slightly and pressed into a loaf pan, bombe or ring mould (mold), re-frozen then turned out and decorated before serving.

◆ GRAND MARNIER PARFAIT ◆

◇ PREPARATION ◇

◇ Stir the sugar into the water over a medium heat until it has dissolved. Add the orange rind, bring the syrup to the boil and continue to boil rapidly for 5 minutes.

◇ Whisk the egg yolks until they are very thick and light in colour. Slowly pour on the syrup, whisking constantly. Continue whisking until the mixture is thick again and cool.

◇ Beat the cream until it is just beginning to thicken. Carefully fold into the egg mixture, starting with just one spoonful and gradually adding the remainder. Flavour with Grand Marnier.

◇ Pour the parfait into a soufflé dish, mould (mold) or loaf pan and freeze until firm. It does not need to be stirred. If you are using a soufflé dish, tie a paper collar around the outside to come at least 5 cm/ 2 inches above the top of the dish to give the impression that it has risen. Transfer the parfait to the refrigerator 30 minutes before serving, sieve (sift) a little cocoa over the top to give a browned finish and remove the collar.

◇ If you have used a mould (mold) or loaf pan, rub a warm, damp cloth over the surface of the mould (mold) or pan and turn the parfait onto an attractive serving dish. Sprinkle with cocoa as above or decorate with whipped cream and pieces of orange, either fresh, caramelized or brandied (see page 119).

VARIATION Line a mould (mold), loaf pan or soufflé dish with sponge fingers, sprinkle with liqueur and then pour over the parfait mixture. Turn out before serving. Alternatively, if using a soufflé dish, arrange the sponge fingers over the top of the frozen parfait so that they look like the spokes of a wheel. Sprinkle with cocoa as above.

The grated rind of a lime can also be added to the syrup above and the parfait flavoured with Benedictine rather than Grand Marnier. The basic parfait can be flavoured in any number of ways by substituting different liqueurs, and using fruit or nut purées, melted chocolate, or coffee. The mixture can also be divided into three or four bowls, each given a different flavour, and then frozen in layers for a multi-coloured effect. Place one batch at a time in the dish or mould (mold), freeze until just firm and then pour the next batch on top.

◇ INGREDIENTS ◇

SERVES 8

¾ cup/175 g/6 oz sugar

⅓ cup/75 ml/2½ fl oz water

15 ml/1 tbsp finely grated orange rind

6 egg yolks

2½ cups/575 ml/1 pt double (heavy) cream

⅓ cup/75 ml/2½ fl oz Grand Marnier

KULFI (INDIAN ICE CREAM)

◇ INGREDIENTS ◇

SERVES 8

4 cups/950 ml/32 fl oz milk

15 ml/1 tbsp arrowroot

¼ cup/50 g/2 oz sugar

½ cup/125 ml/4 fl oz double (heavy) cream

3 cardamom pods

15 ml/1 tbsp chopped almonds or pistachios

few drops rose water

◇ PREPARATION ◇

◇ Bring a quarter of the milk to the boil in a wide, shallow pan. Keep it on the boil, stirring constantly, until it is very thick. Most of it will evaporate but this is as it should be. The length of time it takes for the milk to thicken depends on the surface area of your pan — the wider the pan, the faster the milk will thicken. Set aside until it is completely cold.

◇ Mix some of the remaining milk with the arrowroot to make a paste. Add one of the cardamom pods to the rest of the milk and bring to the boil. Keep boiling, stirring constantly, for 10 minutes. Remove the cardamom pod. Add the arrowroot paste and continue stirring until the milk has thickened.

◇ Stir the sugar into the hot milk until it has dissolved.

◇ Remove the seeds from the remaining cardamom pods, crush them and stir into the milk.

◇ Stir in the chopped nuts. Leave the milk to cool, stirring occasionally.

◇ Whisk the cream until it is stiff enough to hold its shape. Gently fold into the cooled milk, starting with just one spoonful and gradually adding the remainder. Stir in the cooled thickened milk which was made earlier and add the few drops of rose water.

◇ Pour the Kulfi into a freezer tray or plastic box, cover and freeze for 1–2 hours. Beat well and return to the freezer. Beat again every 2 hours until the ice cream is firm.

CHAPTER THREE

Sundaes and Milkshakes

ONCE domestic refrigeration became the norm it was only a short step to bringing ice cream home from the sweet shop (candy store) or supermarket. And once the ice cream was at home, it was no longer a luxury, but an everyday affair. It has always been a standby for unexpected visitors, especially on those days when there was no time to make a dessert. Anyone with ice cream in the freezer can instantly create an exotic sundae, cake, pie or shake. Procope, Escoffier and Lenôtre, great chefs of their day, created confections which were named after famous dancers and artists such as Dame Nellie Melba and Anna Pavlova. More recently, Baskin Robbins have organized 'Show-Off' competitions and the entries poured in. We can't all cook, but we can – and do – make milkshakes and sundaes!

Ice cream, sherbet and sorbets are so very versatile that although certain popular sundaes are to be found on virtually every restaurant menu, there are endless new ideas and recipes constantly being created. So much scope exists for combinations of ingredients that it is not at all unusual to find sundaes on offer for groups – everyone has a spoon and digs into a huge bowl set in the middle of the table.

As for drinks, a little of what you fancy can go a long, long way. Fresh fruit, yogurt, cocktails can all be whizzed together in no time at all. Shakes are filling when you want something between meals, refreshing when you want a long drink.

There is a social history to the sundae and milkshake as well. While slowly nibbling a sundae or sipping a milkshake or ice cream soda in a café, ice cream parlour, or diner you can see and be seen, chatting amiably and enjoying both the company and the refreshment.

◆ *KNICKERBOCKER GLORY* ◆

◇ *I N G R E D I E N T S* ◇
SERVES 4
1 packet red jelly (Jello)
1 packet yellow jelly (Jello)
1 packet green jelly (Jello)
2 cups/450 ml/16 fl oz ice cream
½ cup/125 ml/4 fl oz double (heavy) or whipping cream
20 ml/4 tsp chocolate strands
4 glacé (candied) or Maraschino cherries

◇ *P R E P A R A T I O N* ◇

◇ Make up each jelly (Jello) according to the instructions on the packet (package) and leave to set in separate dishes. When they have set completely, dice into small pieces. Use any flavour combination you like, but remember that the important thing is to use contrasting colours. You will have more jelly than you need for four sundaes — use as much or as little as you like. To make your own jelly, see page 121.

◇ A Knickerbocker Glory should always be served in a tall glass so that the different layers can be seen. Place a few cubes of red jelly in the bottom of the glass, top with a scoop of ice cream then cubes of green jelly, more ice cream and cubes of yellow jelly. Finish with another scoop of ice cream. Use any flavour — onc or more varieties — that you like.

◇ Whisk the cream until it is stiff and pile or pipe onto the ice cream.

◇ Sprinkle with chocolate strands and crown with a cherry.

VARIATION Drizzle 15 ml/1 tbsp Marshmallow or Chocolate Sauce over the top scoop of ice cream.

◆ BANANA SPLIT ◆

◇ INGREDIENTS ◇

SERVES 4

4 medium bananas

2 cups/450 ml/16 fl oz ice cream

½ cup/125 g/4 oz crushed pineapple

½ cup/125 g/4 oz crushed raspberries

½ cup/125 ml/4 fl oz chocolate sauce (see page 125)

½ cup/125 ml/4 fl oz double (heavy) or whipping cream

8 Maraschino or glacé (candied) cherries

⅓ cup/50 g/2 oz flaked or chopped nuts

◇ PREPARATION ◇

◇ Cut the bananas in half lengthways and place two halves on opposite sides of each serving dish.

◇ The ice cream can be any flavour you choose, and a Banana Split is all the better for having two or three flavours of ice cream. Place three scoops of ice cream on each dish, between the banana halves.

◇ Carefully spoon the fruit over two of the scoops of ice cream and the chocolate sauce over the remaining scoop.

◇ Whisk the cream until it is stiff and pile or pipe it on top of the Banana Split. Decorate with chopped cherries and toasted or chopped nuts.

VARIATION Substitute Marshmallow Sauce (see page 126) for chocolate sauce, or, for a truly gooey sundae, use both. The pineapple and raspberries can be left out or replaced by any other fruit you prefer.

◆ *MELON FRAPPE* ◆

◇ INGREDIENTS ◇

SERVES 4

2 medium melons

1¼ cup/500 ml/½ pt sugar syrup

¼ cup/50 ml/2 fl oz Kirsch, Maraschino, port or sherry

◇ PREPARATION ◇

◇ Cut the melons in half and carefully remove the seeds. Scoop out the pulp but be sure not to damage the shells of the melon. Set these aside.

◇ Use the fruit from one of the melons to make a sorbet (sherbet).

◇ Dice the fruit of the remaining melon and soak it in the alcohol.

◇ To assemble the Frappe, place alternate layers of fruit pieces and scoops of sorbet (sherbet) in each half of the melon. Finish with sorbet (sherbet). Brush the outside of the melon shells with water and return to the freezer until 15 minutes before serving.

◇ Melon Frappes can be served either as desserts or starters.

VARIATION Use only one melon and alternate the layers of fruit with a sharp Cranberry Sorbet (Sherbet) (see page 85).

The melons can be whatever type are available, and various kinds can be combined. For example, one cantaloupe and one honeydew melon. Alternatively, one very large melon can be used for serving, filled with fruit from one or more types of melon plus pieces of pineapple, orange, mango, strawberries or any other appealing fruit, with different kinds of sorbet (sherbet) or ice cream.

◆ COUPE JACQUES ◆

◇ INGREDIENTS ◇

SERVES 4

60 ml/4 tbsp diced, fresh fruit

30 ml/2 tbsp sugar syrup or Kirsch

1 cup/250 ml/8 fl oz lemon ice cream

1 cup/250 ml/8 fl oz strawberry ice cream

◇ PREPARATION ◇

◇ Leave the fruit in a bowl with the syrup or Kirsch for 1 hour. Any kind of fruit, in any combination can be used.

◇ Place a scoop each of the lemon and strawberry ice creams in each sundae dish or wine glass. Top with a spoonful of fruit. If there is any syrup or Kirsch left in the bowl, divide it among the sundaes. Decorate with whipped cream and crystallized fruit.

VARIATION The combination above is a classic Coupe Jacques, but any other flavours of ice cream, fruit and liqueur can be used, according to taste and availability. Fruit soaked in some kind of alcohol, a contrasting or complimenting kind of ice cream and a topping of whipped cream with a decorative garnish are the important ingredients to remember. The cream can be plain or sweetened with vanilla sugar.

PEACH CARDINAL ◆

◇ *I N G R E D I E N T S* ◇

SERVES 4

¾ cup/175 g/6 oz sugar

1 cup/250 ml/8 fl oz water

1 vanilla pod (optional)

2 large peaches

2 cups/450 ml/16 fl oz strawberry ice cream

60 ml/4 tbsp redcurrant jelly

15 ml/1 tbsp Kirsch

◇ *P R E P A R A T I O N* ◇

◇ Stir the sugar in the water over a medium heat until it has dissolved.

◇ Add the split vanilla pod if you are using it. Alternatively, use sugar that has been stored with a vanilla pod in it.

◇ Plunge the peaches in boiling water for 2 minutes then remove and skin. Cut in half and carefully remove the stones. Poach in the syrup until tender. Leave to cool in the syrup.

◇ Whisk the redcurrant jelly with the Kirsch until it is smooth.

◇ To assemble the Peach Cardinal, place two scoops of ice cream in each serving dish. Top with a peach half, rounded side up and top with a spoonful of redcurrant jelly.

◆ PEACH MELBA ◆

◇ INGREDIENTS ◇

SERVES 4

1½ cups/250 g/8 oz raspberries

½ lemon

¼ cup/50 g/2 oz sugar

30 ml/2 tbsp gin, Kirsch or Cointreau (optional)

2 large peaches

2 cups/450 ml/16 fl oz vanilla ice cream

◇ PREPARATION ◇

◇ Simmer the raspberries with the juice of the lemon and the sugar for 5 minutes. Stir constantly to be sure that the sugar is thoroughly dissolved. Cool slightly and sieve (strain) to remove all the pips (seeds). Add any alcohol to the sauce at this stage and set aside to cool.

◇ Plunge the peaches in boiling water for 2 minutes then remove and skin. Cut in half and carefully remove the stones. The peaches can be used fresh or, if you prefer, poached in a vanilla syrup which is widely available.

◇ Leave until completely cool if you are cooking them.

◇ To assemble the peach Melba, place two scoops of ice cream in each serving dish. Top with a peach half, rounded side up, and carefully pour the raspberry sauce over the top.

◆ PEARS HELENE ◆

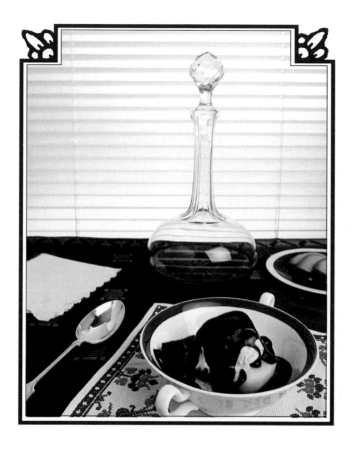

◇ INGREDIENTS ◇

SERVES 4

¾ cup/175 g/6 oz sugar

1 cup/250 ml/8 fl oz water

1 vanilla pod (optional)

2 large pears

1 cup/250 g/8 oz plain (dark) chocolate pieces

1 cup/250 ml/8 fl oz water

½ cup/125 g/4 oz butter

2 cups/450 ml/16 fl oz vanilla ice cream

◇ PREPARATION ◇

◇ Stir the sugar in 1 cup/250 ml/8 fl oz of water over a medium heat until it has dissolved.

◇ Add the split vanilla pod if you are using it. Alternatively, use sugar that has been stored with a vanilla pod in it.

◇ Peel the pears, cut in half and carefully remove the core. Place the pears in the syrup and simmer gently until they are tender. Cool in the syrup.

◇ Melt the chocolate and 1 cup/250 ml/8 fl oz of water together, mixing occasionally, until smooth and thoroughly blended. Cut the butter into small pieces and stir in until the sauce is smooth.

◇ To assemble the pears Hélène, drain the fruit well and place one half in each serving dish. Top with a scoop of ice cream and carefully pour the hot chocolate sauce over the top.

VARIATION Substitute ¼ cup/50 ml/2 fl oz single (light) cream for half of the butter in the chocolate sauce.

◆ CHOCOLATE LIEGOIS ◆

◇ INGREDIENTS ◇

SERVES 4

2 cups/450 ml/16 fl oz chocolate ice cream

1 quantity Chocolate Sauce recipe

1/2 cup/125 ml/4 fl oz double (heavy) or whipping cream

20 ml/4 tsp chocolate strands

4 glacé (candied) or Maraschino cherries

◇ PREPARATION ◇

◇ Assemble the sundae in a tall glass or sundae dish if possible, although a shallow dish or coupe is a good second choice. Place two scoops of the chocolate ice cream in each glass or dish, pour the sauce over the ice cream and top with whipped cream, chocolate strands and a cherry. In France, the sundae would have a paper parasol or flaming sparkler as a finishing touch. Liègois are traditionally very sweet and sticky, with a great deal of cream.

VARIATION Use different kinds of ice cream with a complimentary sauce. For example, coffee ice cream and sauce, vanilla ice cream with crushed pineapple or peaches, strawberry or raspberry ice cream with raspberry sauce go together well.

◆ CHRISTMAS SUNDAE ◆

◇ INGREDIENTS ◇

SERVES 4

2 cups/450 ml/16 fl oz vanilla ice cream
(see pages 14 and 16)

1 cup/225 ml/8 oz mincemeat

15 ml/1 tbsp rum or brandy

◇ PREPARATION ◇

◇ Place two scoops of ice cream in each dish.
◇ Stir the rum or brandy into the mincemeat and heat through gently.
◇ Spoon over the ice cream and serve immediately.

VARIATION Substitute an orange or lemon sorbet (sherbet) for the ice cream, or soften the ice cream, mix with a chestnut, coffee or chocolate purée and re-freeze until ready for serving.

OPPOSITE: Chocolate Liègois
(*see* above)

◆ PARTY SUNDAE ◆

◇ INGREDIENTS ◇

SERVES 8

3³/4 cups/900 ml/1¹/2 pt ice cream

approx. 2 cups/450 ml/16 oz fruit

1–1¹/2 cups/225 ml/8 oz nuts

2 cups/450 ml/16 fl oz sauce

whipped cream

chocolate strands

glacé or Maraschino cherries

◇ PREPARATION ◇

◇   A party sundae should ideally have as much variety as possible so that each person can fill their dish with whatever combination they fancy. The ice cream can include one or more sorbets (sherbets) for contrast and should include at least two different kinds, but preferably even more. To make the selection look particularly attractive, scoop the ice cream into balls several hours before your guests are due.

Roll some of the scoops in a variety of coatings — chocolate strands, chopped nuts, toasted coconut, biscuit (cookie) or wafer crumbs are just a few of the options. Place the scoops on a tray or a sheet of greaseproof (waxed) paper and return to the freezer until you are ready to assemble the sundaes.

◇   The fruit can be a combination of fresh, tinned (canned) or poached, cooked in either apple juice, sugar syrup or alcohol and can be crushed or served in sections.

◇   The nuts can be chopped or flaked, plain or toasted. Use a combination of peanuts, coconut, pistachios, almonds, walnuts or pecans.

◇   Use at least one fruit sauce plus two others such as chocolate, coffee, marshmallow or butterscotch. They can be either hot or cold, or a combination. A choice of liqueurs can also be offered.

◇   Wafers, biscuits (cookies), meringues, marshmallows, mints or any other kind of candy can also be served. The most important thing is to make the selection as interesting and attractive as possible.

◇   Top with a mound of cream and crown with a cherry.

◆ BANANA FLAMBE ◆

◇ INGREDIENTS ◇

SERVES 4

2 cups/450 ml/16 fl oz vanilla ice cream

4 bananas

5 tbsp/60 g/2½ oz butter

5 tbsp/60 g/2½ oz brown sugar

1 lime

2 oranges

¼ cup/50 ml/2 fl oz Grand Marnier or rum

◇ PREPARATION ◇

◇　Slice the bananas in half lengthways. Brown to desired softness in the melted butter. Remove the bananas and place two halves in each dish. Top with two scoops of ice cream.

◇　Stir the sugar into the butter over a gentle heat, until it has dissolved. Add the juice of the lime and oranges. When the sauce is bubbling, heat the Grand Marnier or rum, add to the sauce and set alight. Pour over the ice cream and serve immediately.

VARIATIONS Use ginger ice cream and stir 2 knobs of diced preserved stem ginger into the sauce. Substitute peach or pineapple slices for the bananas.

　Enliven the sauce with 15 ml/1 tbsp orange flower water.

◆ CHERRIES JUBILEE ◆

◇ INGREDIENTS ◇

SERVES 4

2 cups/450 ml/16 fl oz ice cream

1 cup/225 g/8 oz black cherries

15 ml/1 tbsp sugar

15 ml/1 tbsp cornflour (cornstarch)

1 cup/225 ml/8 fl oz fruit juice or water

¼ cup/50 ml/2 fl oz brandy

◇ PREPARATION ◇

◇ Use vanilla, cherry or orange ice cream or cherry, orange or lemon sorbet (sherbet). A yogurt-based ice cream can also be used — its tart flavour makes a superb contrast with the fruit sauce.

◇ Arrange scoops of ice cream or sorbet (sherbet) in a large glass serving dish.

◇ Drain and stone (pit) the cherries.

◇ Combine the sugar and cornflour (cornstarch). Stir in the fruit juice or water and heat gently until the sauce has thickened. Add the cherries and heat for 3–4 minutes.

◇ Warm the brandy, pour it over the cherry sauce and set alight. Pour the sauce over the ice cream and serve immediately.

VARIATION Substitute red wine for the fruit juice and sharpen with a spoonful of lemon juice. Use Kirsch instead of brandy.

◆ ICE CREAM SODAS ◆ CHOCOLATE SYRUP ◆

◇ INGREDIENTS ◇

SERVES 1

30 ml/2 tbsp chocolate, coffee or fruit syrup

¼ cup/50 ml/2 fl oz milk

½ cup/125 ml/4 fl oz ice cream

½ cup/125 ml/4 fl oz soda water (club soda)

whipped cream

chocolate strands

glacé or Maraschino cherry

◇ PREPARATION ◇

◇ Combine the syrup and milk in the bottom of a very tall glass. Mix until smooth.

◇ Add two scoops of any kind of ice cream.

◇ Fill the glass with soda water (club soda) and mix gently with a long spoon. Any flavoured soda you like can be used.

◇ Top with a mound of whipped cream, sprinkle on some chocolate strands and crown with a cherry.

◇ INGREDIENTS ◇

MAKES 1 CUP/225 ML/8 FL OZ

½ cup/5 g/2 oz unsweetened cocoa

1 cup/225 g/8 oz sugar

pinch salt

1 cup/225 ml/8 fl oz boiling water

2½ ml/½ tsp vanilla essence (extract)

◇ PREPARATION ◇

◇ Combine the cocoa, sugar and salt. Stir in the boiling water. Cook over a medium heat, stirring constantly, until thick and smooth. Flavour with vanilla essence (extract).

◇ Store the syrup in a covered jar as it will make enough for several desserts.

◆ *PARTY PUNCH* ◆

◇ *I N G R E D I E N T S* ◇

SERVES 10—12

2 bottles sweet or sparkling white wine

3¾ cups/675 ml/1½ pt sorbet (sherbet)

◇ *P R E P A R A T I O N* ◇

◇ Place small scoops of several different kinds of sorbet (sherbet) in a large bowl, pour the wine over the top and serve in punch glasses.

VARIATIONS Mix champagne and orange juice to make a 'Buck's Fizz', or Cassis and white wine to make 'Kir'. Pour over the sorbet (sherbet).

Whole pieces of fruit — strawberries, raspberries, peaches, apricots, melon — can be added to the punch so that each cup contains a scoop of sherbet, a piece of fruit and some alcohol.

Use red wine instead of white for a claret cup.

Add brandy or any liqueur to taste. If you want the punch to go further, add sparkling mineral water, soda water (club soda) or orange juice. The larger the quantity you mix, the better the punch will be as it improves with a wide range of ingredients.

If you want to prepare the sorbet (sherbet) in advance, make the scoops, place on a tray lined with greaseproof (waxed) paper and return to the freezer until just before your guests arrive.

To make an exotic-looking punch, serve it in a hollowed out watermelon shell, or serve individual drinks in smaller melon shells, orange or pineapple shells or even a hollow coconut! The simplest way of serving individual drinks is to pour a measure of liqueur or spirit into the bottom of a champagne flute or brandy snifter, add a scoop of sorbet (sherbet) or ice cream and top with either sparkling white wine, red wine, or the fruit juice or soda of your choice. If the drink is for children, simply omit the alcohol at the bottom of the glass.

◆ *MILKSHAKES* ◆

◆ *CHOCOLATE MILKSHAKE* ◆

◇ I N G R E D I E N T S ◇

SERVES 4

60 ml/4 tbsp chocolate syrup

2½ cups/575 ml/1 pt milk

1 cup/225 ml/8 fl oz chocolate ice cream (see page 21)

◇ P R E P A R A T I O N ◇

◇ Combine the syrup, milk and ice cream in a liquidizer, blender or food processor.

◇ Mix until smooth and frothy. Pour into large glasses, and garnish with whipped cream, grated chocolate or a marshmallow.

◇ Any variation of chocolate ice cream — mocha, mint, cherry — may be substituted for plain chocolate ice cream.

◆ *BANANA MILKSHAKE* ◆

◇ I N G R E D I E N T S ◇

SERVES 4

4 bananas

3¾ cups/900 ml/1½ pt milk

1 cup/225 ml/8 fl oz ice cream

◇ P R E P A R A T I O N ◇

◇ Peel and chop the bananas. Combine with the milk and ice cream in a liquidizer, blender or food processor until smooth and frothy. The ice cream can be vanilla, banana, chocolate, pineapple or any kind, according to taste. Pour into large glasses and serve sprinkled with grated chocolate.

◆ ICED GRASSHOPPER ◆

◇ INGREDIENTS ◇

SERVES 4

2 cups/450 ml/16 fl oz mint or pistachio ice cream
(see page 20)

¼ cup/50 ml/2 fl oz Crème de Menthe

¼ cup/50 ml/2 fl oz Crème de Cacao

◇ PREPARATION ◇

◇ Combine all ingredients in a liquidizer, blender or food processor and mix until thick and smooth. Pour into tall glasses and garnish with mint leaves dipped into egg white and sugar to give a frosted appearance.

◆ ICED JULEP ◆

◇ INGREDIENTS ◇

SERVES 4

2 cups/450 ml/16 fl oz mint or vanilla ice cream

¼ cup/50 ml/2 fl oz Crème de Menthe

¼ cup/2 fl oz Southern Comfort or Bourbon

◇ PREPARATION ◇

◇ Combine ingredients in the same way as for Iced Grasshopper . Serve an iced julep over crushed ice and garnish with a sprig of mint.

◆ *FROZEN LATIN FLIP* ◆

◆ *DOWN HOME SHAKE* ◆

◇ I N G R E D I E N T S ◇

S E R V E S 4

*2 cups/450 ml/16 fl oz coffee, rum or chocolate ice cream
(see page 21)*

*1/2 cup/125 ml/4 fl oz Tia Maria, Kahlua or
Crème de Cacao*

1 cup/225 ml/8 fl oz milk

◇ P R E P A R A T I O N ◇

◇ As for iced grasshopper. Garnish with chocolate strands.

◇ I N G R E D I E N T S ◇

S E R V E S 4

*2 cups/450 ml/16 fl oz chocolate, rum or ginger ice cream,
or lemon sorbet (sherbet) (see pages 21, 29)*

15 ml/1 tbsp honey

1/4 cup/50 ml/2 fl oz dark rum

1 cup/225 ml/8 fl oz milk

◇ P R E P A R A T I O N ◇

◇ Combine ingredients in the same way as for iced grasshopper (see page 58). Omit the mint leaf garnish but serve with either grated chocolate or a sprinkling of cinnamon or ground ginger on top.

◆ FRESH FRUIT SHAKES ◆

◇ *INGREDIENTS* ◇

SERVES 4

1 cup/225 g/8 oz fresh fruit

3¾ cups/900 ml/1½ pt milk

1 cup/225 ml/8 fl oz ice cream or sorbet (sherbet)

◇ *PREPARATION* ◇

◇ Any soft fruit can be used for delicious milk-shakes — try raspberry, strawberry, peach, apricot or pineapple. Crush or purée the fruit, add the milk and a complimentary kind of ice cream or sorbet (sherbet). Transfer this to a liquidizer, blender or food processor and mix until smooth and frothy. Serve in large glasses, garnished with a piece of the whole fruit.

VARIATION Partially defrosted frozen fruit, or well drained tinned (canned) fruit can be used in the same way.

For a very sweet milkshake, use ½ cup/125 g/4 oz of jam or fruit preserve instead of whole fruit.

Alternatively, use fruit juice instead of milk to mix with the whole fruit and ice cream. Any combination of several kinds of fruit with orange, apple or pineapple juice and the ice cream or sorbet (sherbet) of your choice will create a delicious shake.

A splash of liqueur to go with the fruit will also enhance the fresh fruit shake. Super thick shakes can be made with more ice cream and less liquid.

◆ YOGURT SHAKES ◆

◇ *INGREDIENTS* ◇

SERVES 4

1¼ cups/300 ml/10 oz yogurt

2½ cups/575 ml/1 pt milk

1 cup/225 ml/8 fl oz ice cream or sorbet (sherbet)

◇ *PREPARATION* ◇

◇ Use any variety of yogurt and ice cream or sorbet (sherbet) you have available.

◇ Combine with the milk in a liquidizer, blender or food processor and mix until smooth and frothy.

◆ *FROZEN DAIQUIRI* ◆ *CARIBBEAN FLIP* ◆

◇ *INGREDIENTS* ◇

SERVES 4

½ cup/125 g/4 oz 2.5-cm/1-inch ice cubes

½ cup/125 ml/4 fl oz white rum

2 cups/450 ml/16 fl oz sorbet (sherbet) or ice cream

½ cup/125 g/4 oz fresh fruit

◇ *PREPARATION* ◇

◇ Crush the ice and mix with the rum and sorbet (sherbet) or ice cream in a liquidizer, blender or food processor. Add the fruit and mix until thick and frothy.

◇ Use either fresh fruit ice cream (raspberry, strawberry, apricot, pineapple or banana for example) or a white wine or cider sorbet (sherbet) and a complementary fruit for the Daiquiri.

◇ *INGREDIENTS* ◇

SERVES 4

2 cups/450 ml/16 fl oz rum or chocolate ice cream (see page 21)

1 cup/225 ml/8 fl oz milk

10 ml/2 tsp instant coffee

½ cup/125 ml/4 fl oz dark rum or brandy

10 ml/2 tsp Cointreau or Curaçao

◇ *PREPARATION* ◇

◇ Combine the ingredients in same way as for iced grasshopper (see page 58). Garnish with a stick of cinnamon or a sprinkling of ground cinnamon and a twist of orange peel.

◆ SORBET (SHERBET) MULLED WINE ◆ SPICED CIDER CUP ◆

◇ *INGREDIENTS* ◇	◇ *INGREDIENTS* ◇
SERVES 12—15	SERVES 8
2 bottles red wine	*7½ cups/1½ l/3 pt cider*
2 oranges	*¼ cup/50 g/2 oz brown sugar*
1 lemon	*1 stick cinnamon*
1 stick cinnamon	*3 cloves*
pinch ground nutmeg	*2½ ml/½ tsp allspice*
1¼ cups/300 ml/10 fl oz boiling water	*2 cups/450 ml/16 fl oz sorbet (sherbet), apple, orange or*
¼ cup/50 ml/2 fl oz brandy or Cointreau (optional)	*lemon (see pages 85 and 86)*
2 cups/450 ml/16 fl oz sorbet (sherbet)	*ground nutmeg*

◇ *PREPARATION* ◇

◇ Heat the wine with the sliced oranges and lemon, cinnamon and nutmeg until just below boiling temperature. Simmer for 15 minutes. Add the boiling water and the brandy or Cointreau if you are using it.

◇ Ladle the wine into glasses and add a scoop of sorbet (sherbet) — use orange or lemon — or a contrasting white wine sorbet (sherbet).

◇ *PREPARATION* ◇

◇ Stir the sugar into the cider over a medium heat until it is completely dissolved. Add the spices and simmer for 10 minutes.

◇ Remove the spices and ladle the cider into glasses. Add a scoop of sorbet (sherbet). Top with a sprinkling of nutmeg.

◆ *CARIBBEAN COFFEE* ◆

◇ *I N G R E D I E N T S* ◇

SERVES 4

2¹/₂ cups/575 ml/1 pt strong black coffee

1 cup/225 ml/8 fl oz ice cream, vanilla, chocolate, ginger,
OR *coffee (see pages 14, 16, 21 and 29)*

60 ml/4 tbsp rum sauce (see page 126)

◇ *P R E P A R A T I O N* ◇

◇ Ladle the hot coffee into cups, add a scoop of the ice cream and top with a spoonful of rum sauce.

◆ *HOT CHOCOLATE FLOAT* ◆

◇ *I N G R E D I E N T S* ◇

SERVES 4

3³/₄ cups/900 ml/1¹/₂ pt milk

¹/₄ cup/50 g/2 oz plain (dark) chocolate

5 ml/1 tsp vanilla essence (extract)

*1 cup/225 ml/8 fl oz ice cream, vanilla or chocolate
(see pages 14, 16 and 21)*

whipped cream

2¹/₂ ml/¹/₂ tsp cinnamon (optional)

◇ *P R E P A R A T I O N* ◇

◇ Heat the milk with the broken chocolate until it has melted. Whisk and add the vanilla essence (extract).

◇ Pour the chocolate into cups, add a scoop of the ice cream and top with whipped cream. Sprinkle cinnamon on top of each portion and serve immediately.

VARIATION
10 ml/2 tsp instant coffee
3³/₄ cups/900 ml/1¹/₂ pt milk
30 ml/2 tbsp unsweetened cocoa
30 ml/2 tbsp sugar or honey
¹/₂ cup/125 ml/4 fl oz boiling water

◇ Stir the coffee into the hot milk until it has dissolved.

◇ Dissolve the cocoa and sugar or honey in the water. Mix into the milk and proceed as above.

RIGHT: Caribbean Coffee
LEFT: Hot Chocolate Float

Ice Cream Dishes

 THE RANGE of commercial ice creams has expanded in all kinds of ways. Neapolitans, cassata and bombes opened a new world of desserts. The variations on Baked Alaska (Omelette [Omelet] en Surprise) and Vacherin now vie for position with gâteaux, choux buns, and galettes.

Although the masterpieces wheeled out at aristocratic banquets during the previous century cannot be surpassed by modern-day creations, today's methods of cooking have given rise to their own innovations. For example, an Oxford University professor of Physics, Nicholas Kurti, with a special interest in food and cooking, recently demonstrated that a 'reverse' Baked Alaska is possible. He sealed a portion of jam inside a brick of ice cream and found that by cooking the dish in a specially converted microwave oven the jam got hot while the ice cream remained cold! The possible variations from this experiment could grow enormously.

Presentation has also taken on new meaning in recent years. Sauces are arranged in beautiful patterns on decorative plates and topped with scoops of sorbet (sherbet) in a Nouvelle Cuisine style. Tiny spoonfuls of sorbet (sherbet) may often be effectively interspersed with pieces of fruit or flowers and leaves. Unusually shaped and coloured dishes, glasses and bowls supplement the traditional coupes and parfait glasses. Edible baskets are made from freshly baked biscuits (cookies), shaped while hot to make *tulipes*. Meringues, choux pastry, flan cases (pie shells), and biscuit (cookie) crumb crusts, chocolate or syrup coated breakfast cereal, round or rectangular sponges, angel food cakes and giant biscuits (cookies) are all used as cases to be filled or layered with ice cream.

Frozen food cabinets and snack bars introduce young people to a fine art in creating ice cream dishes and ideas, which they develop over a lifetime. The recipes that follow include a few of the classics and a few innovations – take it from there!

◆ ICE CREAM BOMBE ◆

◇ INGREDIENTS ◇

SERVES 8—10

1¼ cups/300 ml/10 fl oz coffee ice cream (see page 14)

1¼ cups/300 ml/10 fl oz pecan or almond ice cream (see page 20)

¼ cup/50 g/2 oz plain (dark) chocolate pieces

2 eggs

30 ml/2 tbsp Tia Maria, Crème de Cacao or Cointreau

30 ml/2 tbsp brandy

¼ cup/50 ml/2 fl oz double (heavy) cream

◇ PREPARATION ◇

◇ Soften the coffee ice cream slightly and spread over the inside of a chilled 2½ pt/1 l mould (mold). The mould (mold) should be metal if possible. If you use a plastic bowl or mould (mold) line with plastic wrap, leaving a 5 cm/2 inch overlap. This will make it easier to remove the frozen bombe. Freeze for 30 minutes.

◇ Soften the pecan or almond ice cream and spread over the coffee ice cream to make a second layer. Freeze for 30 minutes.

◇ While the ice creams are freezing, prepare the mousse filling: melt the broken chocolate in the top of a double boiler. Add the lightly beaten eggs and mix well. Add the liqueur and brandy. Leave to cool.

◇ Whisk the cream until it is just beginning to thicken. Carefully fold into the chocolate mixture.

◇ Fill the centre of the bombe with the mousse. Cover the surface with a circle of greaseproof (waxed) paper, cover the mould (mold) and freeze. When you are ready to serve the bombe, dip the mould (mold) into a bowl of hot water, loosen the edge with a pallette knife (metal spatula) and invert onto a serving dish. Return to the freezer for a few minutes to keep it firm and then decorate quickly

before serving. The garnish can be piped cream, angelica or glacé (candied) cherries, toasted nuts, grated chocolate or pieces of fruit.

VARIATIONS Again, there are limitless variations to this recipe. Try some of the following ideas.

Maple walnut ice cream, coffee ice cream with a filling of butterscotch sauce lightened with whipped cream.

Vanilla ice cream only, half of it being mixed with pieces of fruit soaked in rum, sherry or Kirsch, or diced marron glacé, chocolate pieces or praline.

Chocolate and vanilla ice cream with a filling of pistachio ice cream, a fruit sorbet or pieces of fruit soaked in brandy or liqueur.

Chocolate and black cherry ice cream with a filling of cherries in Kirsch.

Red fruit ice cream (raspberry, strawberry or blackcurrant) plus a layer of claret sorbet (sherbet) and a filling of crushed fruit.

Peach or apricot ice cream plus a layer of white wine or champagne sorbet (sherbet) and a filling of crushed fruit or diced dried fruit soaked in wine.

Coffee or chocolate and almond ice cream with a filling of chestnut mousse.

One important point to remember when making a bombe is that it should not only taste superb, but should look tempting when it is cut, so try to use contrasting colours and different kinds of ice cream and fillings. A custard based ice cream is most suitable for the two outer layers. The innermost layer should be totally different in texture and nature; either a sorbet (sherbet), a mousse, crushed fruit mixed with liqueur, crushed meringues or macaroons mixed with liqueur or a flavoured cream mixed with chopped glacé (candied) fruit.

After the innermost layer has been frozen for 1 hour, the bombe can be removed from the freezer and sealed with either a round of cake or one more layer of ice cream.

◆ CASSATA ◆

◇ INGREDIENTS ◇

SERVES 8

2 cups/450 ml/16 fl oz strawberry ice cream (see page 24)

1/4 cup/50 g/2 oz pistachio nuts

1/4 cup/50 g/2 oz glacé (candied) cherries

1/4 cup/50 g/2 oz raisins

30 ml/2 tbsp brandy or liqueur

1/4 cup/50 g/2 oz chocolate drops

2 cups/450 ml/16 fl oz vanilla ice cream
(see pages 14 and 16)

◇ PREPARATION ◇

◇ Soften the strawberry ice cream slightly and pack it into a loaf pan or brick mould (mold) and then freeze it.

◇ Chop the pistachio nuts and dice the cherries. Soak the cherries and raisins in the brandy or liqueur for 1 hour.

◇ Soften the vanilla ice cream slightly and mix with the nuts, fruit and chocolate drops. Pack into the loaf pan on top of the re-frozen strawberry ice cream and freeze it.

◇ When you are ready to serve the Cassata, turn out of its mould (mold) and slice.

VARIATION To make a Neapolitan ice cream, soften 2 cups/450 ml/16 fl oz of vanilla, strawberry and chocolate ice cream. Pack into a loaf pan, one layer at a time, refreezing after each so that the colours remain separate.

These traditional combinations of ice creams may be successfully replaced by any kind of ice cream, according to availability and personal preference.

◆ EASY ICE CREAM LOAF ◆

◇ INGREDIENTS ◇

SERVES 8

24 Boudoir biscuits (ladies fingers or sponge fingers)

30 ml/2 tbsp Marsala, sherry, brandy, rum, liqueur or fruit juice

2½ cups/575 ml/1 pt ice cream

1 cup/225 ml/8 fl oz double (heavy) cream

30 ml/2 tbsp Coffee, Chocolate, Butterscotch or Fruit sauce

½ cup/50 g/2 oz toasted flaked (slivered) almonds

◇ PREPARATION ◇

◇ Arrange half of the biscuits (ladies fingers) in the base of a loaf pan. Sprinkle with wine, spirit or juice. Soften the ice cream and spread half of it over the biscuits. Repeat with a second layer each of biscuits and ice cream. Cover and freeze for 1 hour or more.

◇ Whisk the cream until it is thick.

◇ Unmould (unmold) the ice cream loaf onto a serving dish. Cover with cream and drizzle the sauce over it. Garnish with flaked (slivered) almonds.

VARIATION Use two different kinds of ice cream or sorbet (sherbet).

Use more ice cream, of several different kinds, and freeze in 20 cm/8 in sandwich cake pans. Assemble the ice cream cake by piling the layers on top of each other. Press boudoir biscuits (ladies fingers) or langues de chat (see page 112) gently around the outside. Top with cream and sauce as above.

◆ BAKED ALASKA ◆

◇ I N G R E D I E N T S ◇

SERVES 8—10

1 sponge cake

45 ml/3 tbsp liqueur (optional)

½ cup/125 g/4 oz fruit, in pieces (optional)

4 egg whites

pinch cream of tartar

½ cup/125 g/4 oz sugar

7½ cups/1½ l/3 pt ice cream

45 ml/3 tbsp icing (confectioners') sugar

oven: 230°C/450°F/Gas 8

◆ BAKED ALASKA ◆

◇ *PREPARATION* ◇

◇ Prepare the sponge cake, cool completely and trim to either a large round, square or rectangular shape. The sponge should be approximately 1 cm/ ½ in thick. Place on an ovenproof dish or tray and sprinkle with the liqueur if you are using it.

◇ Arrange pieces of fruit, if they are being incorporated into the recipe, over the sponge. Any fruit that is complementary to the ice cream can be used.

◇ Whisk the egg whites with the cream of tartar until they are stiff but not dry. Gradually add the sugar, whisking continually until the meringue is stiff again. If the meringue is covered, it can be left for an hour before being used.

◇ To assemble the Baked Alaska, place well frozen ice cream on top of the fruit, or directly on the sponge base if you are not using fruit and trim so that it leaves 1 cm/½ in clear all around. Spoon or pipe the meringue over the surface, and be sure that the cake and ice cream are totally enclosed. Sprinkle the surface with sieved (sifted) icing (confectioners') sugar.

◇ Bake in a preheated oven for 5 minutes, or until the meringue is lightly browned.

◇ Serve immediately.

VARIATION Use a Swiss roll (jelly roll) base instead of the sponge. Sprinkle with liqueur, if you are using it, spread with slightly softened ice cream, top with fruit pieces or purée and roll. Wrap in tin foil. Freeze for 1 hour before enclosing in meringue and baking as above.

Use chocolate cake or an uncut layer of brownies for the base.

Use one large or several individual pastry cases (pie shells) instead of the sponge. Fill with scoops of ice cream and top with meringue. Be sure to seal the case (shell) well. Sprinkle with icing (confectioners') sugar and bake as above.

Fruit Surprise can be made by cutting a slice off the top of a melon, pineapple, orange, lime or grapefruit. Carefully spoon out the fruit leaving the shell intact. Chop the fruit, mix with your favourite liqueur and chill for several hours. Fill the shells with fruit and several scoops of complementary ice cream or sorbet (sherbet). Pile high with meringue. Sprinkle with icing (confectioners') sugar and bake as above.

◆ *PROFITEROLES WITH* ◆ *CHOCOLATE FONDUE SAUCE*

◇ *I N G R E D I E N T S* ◇

SERVES 6

PROFITEROLES

⅔ cup/150 ml/5 fl oz water

¼ cup/50 g/2 oz butter

⅔ cup/65 g/2½ oz flour

pinch salt

2 eggs

CHOCOLATE FONDUE SAUCE

1¼ cups/300 g/10 oz sugar

⅔ cup/150 ml/5 fl oz water

½ cup/125 g/4 oz plain (dark) chocolate, pieces

½ cup/125 g/4 oz milk (light) chocolate, pieces

75 ml/5 tbsp unsalted butter

42½ ml/2½ tbsp double (heavy) cream

75 ml/5 tbsp rum, brandy, Grand Marnier or Cointreau

3 cups/750 g/1¼ pt ice cream

oven: 220°C/425°F/Gas 7

◇ *P R E P A R A T I O N* ◇

◇ Prepare the profiteroles first. Heat the water with the butter until the water has boiled and the butter melted. Sieve (sift) the flour and salt. Add all at once to the water and butter mixture and continue to cook over a moderate heat, stirring constantly, until the pastry forms a ball which leaves the sides of the pan clean. Remove from the heat.

◇ Beat the eggs into the pastry one at a time. Continue to beat until it is shiny and thick enough to hold its shape. Spoon or pipe onto a greased baking tray, making 24 profiteroles.

◇ Bake in a pre-heated oven for 15 minutes. Cool on a wire rack.

◇ To prepare the fondue sauce, heat the sugar with the water over a medium heat until the sugar has dissolved. Leave to cool.

◇ Break the chocolate into small pieces and melt with the cream in the top of a double boiler. Stir occasionally. When the chocolate has melted, slowly add the sugar syrup, stirring constantly. Flavour with the spirit.

◇ Just before you are ready to serve the profiteroles, split them through the middle and fill each with a small scoop of any kind of ice cream, for example vanilla and chocolate, chocolate and cherry. Or, alternatively, use one ice cream and one sorbet (sherbet).

◇ Pile the profiteroles into one large or six small dishes and pour a spoonful of fondue sauce over the top. Serve the remaining sauce separately.

◇ Note: the sauce can be served either hot or cold.

VARIATION Substitute Butterscotch Sauce (page 126) for the Chocolate Fondue Sauce.

◆ BOX OF DELIGHTS ◆

◇ INGREDIENTS ◇

MAKES 8

1 cup/225 ml/8 fl oz ice cream

1 lb/450 g plain (dark) chocolate pieces

½ cup/125 ml/4 fl oz double (heavy) cream

¼–⅓ cup/50 g/2 oz nuts

◇ PREPARATION ◇

◇ Prepare your favourite ice cream and freeze in an ice cube tray so that it is shaped in neat squares. If the ice cream is already made, soften slightly and press into an ice cube tray then re-freeze until you need it.

◇ Melt the chocolate in the top of a double boiler. Stir until it is smooth. Line a Swiss roll (jelly roll) pan with greaseproof (waxed) paper and spread the chocolate over in a thin layer. Leave to set for 30 minutes. Cover with another sheet of greaseproof (waxed) paper and invert. Carefully peel off the lining paper. Cut the chocolate into 32 squares using a very sharp knife.

◇ Place the ice cream cubes on a flat baking sheet lined with greaseproof (waxed) paper. Carefully press four squares of chocolate around each cube. Return to the freezer until it is time to serve.

◇ Whisk the cream until it is stiff. Spoon or pipe onto each box of ice cream and garnish with nuts. Use almonds, walnuts or pecans that have been glazed in a sugar syrup (see page 97), or just sprinkle with chopped pistachios, walnuts or almonds.

VARIATION Prepare a sponge or chocolate cake and bake on a flat tray. When the cake has cooled, cut into squares the size of the ice cream cubes and place one cube on top of each cake square. Brush the sides of the cake with melted apricot jam. Gently press the chocolate squares around each side and proceed as above.

Sweeten the whipped cream, according to taste and add vanilla essence (extract), rum, or a splash of liqueur.

⬧ HAZELNUT GALETTE ⬧

◇ INGREDIENTS ◇

SERVES 8—10

3 eggs (separated)

½ cup/125 g/4 oz sugar

5 ml/1 tsp grated orange or lemon rind

¾ cup/75 g/3 oz ground hazelnuts (filberts)

½ cup/50 g/2 oz potato flour

2½ cups/575 ml/1 pt ice cream

oven: 180°C/350°F/Gas 4

◇ PREPARATION ◇

◇ Whisk the egg yolks with the sugar until thick and light. Fold in the grated rind and the nuts.

◇ Whisk the egg whites until they are stiff but not dry. Fold into the nut mixture, alternating with the sieved (sifted) potato flour.

◇ Spread the batter into two 20 cm/8 in sandwich cake pans. Bake in a preheated oven for 30 minutes. Cool on a wire rack.

◇ Several hours before serving the galette, prepare the ice cream and freeze in a 20 cm/8 in cake pan. If the ice cream is already made, soften slightly, press into a cake pan and re-freeze until firm.

◇ To assemble the galette, place the ice cream between the two 'cakes', like the filling in a sandwich.

VARIATION Use ground walnuts or almonds instead of the hazelnuts (filberts).

Any kind of cake can be used, simply bake in thin layers or slice the layers horizontally.

Use more than two cake layers and more than one kind of ice cream or sorbet (sherbet).

A spoonful of brandy or liqueur can be sprinkled over the cake before assembling.

Bake the cake in a ring shaped pan. Fill the centre with ice cream. Or cut a slice off the top, hollow out and fill with scoops of ice cream. Top with fresh or puréed fruit. Replace the top to make a lid. Ice the cake with a butter frosting and then freeze.

Bake the cake in bun (cupcake) pans, hollow out and fill with ice cream. Or, bake in a Swiss roll (jelly roll) pan, spread with fruit and softened ice cream.

Decorate with whipped cream before freezing.

◆ CRUNCHY ICE CREAM RING ◆

◇ I N G R E D I E N T S ◇

SERVES 6—8

1 cup/225 g/8 oz brown sugar

25 ml/1½ tbsp golden (light corn) syrup

⅓ cup/65 ml/2½ fl oz milk

45 ml/1½ tbsp unsalted (sweet) butter

6 cups/175 g/6 oz cornflakes or rice crispies

2½ cups/575 ml/1 pt ice cream

◇ P R E P A R A T I O N ◇

◇ Heat the sugar and syrup together, stirring constantly, until the sugar has melted. Boil for 3 minutes. Transfer to a large bowl and mix in the milk and butter. Add the cereal and stir, until well coated.

◇ Press the cereal mixture into a greased 20 cm/8 in ring mould (mold). Leave to set. Turn out onto a serving dish and fill the inside of the ring with scoops of ice cream and/or sorbet (sherbet) in any variety of flavours.

VARIATION Use individual ring moulds (molds).

Alternatively, press the mixture into one large or several small pie dishes (plates) or bun (cupcake) pans, leaving a hollow in the middle to fill with ice cream.

◆ CHOCOLATE ICE CREAM RING ◆

◇ I N G R E D I E N T S ◇

SERVES 6—8

¾ cup/175 g/6 oz unsalted (sweet) butter

¾ cup/175 g/6 oz plain (dark) chocolate pieces

¾ cup/175 ml/6 oz golden (light corn) syrup

6 cups/175 g/6 oz cornflakes or rice crispies

2½ cups/575 ml/1 pt ice cream

◇ P R E P A R A T I O N ◇

◇ Melt the butter, chocolate and syrup together. Mix well. Proceed as for Crunchy Ice Cream Ring.

OPPOSITE: Crunchy Ice Cream (right) and Chocolate Ice Cream Ring (left)

◆ *MERINGUE TORTE* ◆

◇ *INGREDIENTS* ◇

SERVES 8—10

4 egg whites

1 cup/225 g/8 oz sugar

2½ cups/575 ml/1 pt ice cream

1 cup/225 ml/8 fl oz double (heavy) cream

16 glazed pecans or walnut halves

oven: 160°C/300°F/Gas 2

◇ *PREPARATION* ◇

◇ Whisk the egg whites until they are stiff. Add the sugar, a spoonful at a time, and continue whisking until the meringue is stiff again. Spoon carefully into a piping (pastry) bag.

◇ Line two flat baking trays with greaseproof (waxed) paper. Trace a 22 cm/9 in circle on each. On one tray, pipe the meringue in rings to fill the entire circle. Smooth the surface with a pallette knife (metal spatula). On the second tray, pipe the meringue in one ring around the inside edge of the circle and then make three parallel lines in each direction to form a lattice.

◇ Bake the meringues in a preheated oven for 30 minutes.

◇ Transfer to a wire cooling rack. When the meringues are completely cold, carefully peel off the lining paper. If you are not using them immediately, store in an airtight container.

◇ Several hours before serving the torte, prepare the ice cream and freeze in a 22 cm/9 in cake pan. If the ice cream is already made, soften slightly, press into a cake pan and re-freeze until firm.

◇ To assemble the torte, place the meringue circle on a serving dish. Top with a layer of ice cream or several layers of different kinds of ice cream.

◇ Whisk the cream until it is stiff and pile on top of the ice cream. Carefully place the lattice meringue on top of the whipped cream. Press down gently so that the cream oozes through the gaps. Place a nut in each gap and serve immediately.

VARIATION Add instant coffee, unsweetened cocoa or ground nuts to the unbaked meringue mixture.

To make a VACHERIN, make one solid layer of meringue only and pipe the remaining mixture onto individual baking trays or sheets to make several rings. When they have been baked, place the solid layer at the bottom and pile the rings on top of each other to make a basket. Make a Swiss meringue (see page 115) and pipe between the layers to seal them and then in vertical lines all around the basket, topping it with a row of rosettes. Bake for 1½ hours until firm. Cool and store until ready to use, then fill with ice cream and top with fresh fruit. Garnish with a fruit sauce.

Sorbets (Sherbets)

A SELECTION of sorbet (sherbet) recipes naturally leads to an interest in the origin of iced desserts. As with much of history, there is a fair amount of debate as to which country initiated the idea. The Greeks and Romans certainly poured honey and syrup over snow from the surrounding mountains, which was brought back by runners, but Marco Polo indubitably brought the idea home with him from China. The Persians and Arabs are also known to have discovered the delights of iced desserts because there are accounts of Alexander the Great ordering his slaves to carry snow home from glaciers, on their return from India.

There is general agreement that the Italians were the fathers of modern European ice cream. When Catherine de Medici wed Henry II of France in 1533, she brought a chef who knew the secret of making ice cream as part of her entourage. From there the concept went to England, to Charles I, although whether his French or Italian chef first introduced it is not known. One legend states that Charles rewarded his chef for not revealing the secret, another that he threatened him with execution if he did.

However, by the seventeenth century ice cream was no longer a Royal secret. Francisco Procopio, another Italian, opened a café in Paris, which was in fact a forerunner to the twentieth century ice cream parlour. Charles II built an 'ice house' in St. James' Park, and aristocrats all over the country followed suit. These were used for storing huge blocks of ice as well as frozen whipped cream and custard. Other European countries used caves, cellars and wells for storing ice. Later, Italian immigrants brought ices to America. The earliest recipes for ice cream had appeared by the middle of the eighteenth century, when ices finally ceased to be the exclusive delight of the rich.

❖ SUGAR SYRUP ❖

◇ INGREDIENTS ◇

SERVES 8

2½ cups/575 ml/1 pt water

1 cup/225 g/8 oz sugar

2 lemons

◇ PREPARATION ◇

◇ Heat the water with the sugar over a medium heat, stirring constantly, until the sugar has dissolved. Boil rapidly for 5 minutes. Stir in the juice and finely grated rind of the lemons. Leave to cool.

FLAVOURING

675 g/1½ lb fresh fruit OR 2½ cups/450 ml/1 pt fruit juice

◇ PREPARATION ◇

◇ Specific appealing combinations of sorbets (sherbets) are given below, but the general method for preparing a sorbet (sherbet) is as follows. There are no hard and fast rules about mixtures, however, which leaves plenty of scope for those who enjoy experimenting.

◇ If the fruit is soft, such as melon or any sort of berry, purée it and sieve it (strain) to remove any seeds and then stir the purée into the sugar syrup (above).

◇ If the fruit is firm, such as peaches, apricots, pears, plums, cherries, it must be cooked before being puréed. Plunge it into boiling water for 2 minutes then remove the skin and stones (pips). Poach in the sugar syrup, white wine or apple juice, cool and purée.

◇ If you decide to use dried fruit, soak it or poach it in water, syrup, fruit juice or wine before puréeing.

◇ If the sorbet is to be made with citrus fruit, finely grate the rind, then squeeze and strain the juice to add to the syrup.

◇ Any additional flavouring may be added — vanilla or almond essence (extract), rose water or orange flower water, wine, liqueur, spirit, cinnamon stick, vanilla pod, ground ginger, coffee, or peppermint leaves.

◇ A combination of several tropical fruits such as cherimoya, mangosteen, passion or kiwi fruit, and persimmon create an exotic sorbet (sherbet).

◇ The lemon juice in the syrup can be omitted and the fruit chosen for the sorbet (sherbet) simply sharpened to taste with 1–2 spoonfuls of lemon juice.

◇ For contrasting textures, soak diced dried or glacé (candied) fruit in spirit for an hour or more and then stir into the partially frozen sorbet (sherbet).

◇ Sorbets (sherbets) should be very smooth and not too solid. Stir several times during freezing, mixing the ice crystals around the outside of the container into the centre. If the sorbet (sherbet) has frozen solid, transfer to the refrigerator for 15–30 minutes before serving.

IDEAS FOR SORBETS (SHERBETS)

add 1¼ cups/300 ml/10 fl oz strong black coffee to the syrup

orange and fresh mint

orange and strawberry

raspberry and redcurrant

plums and gin

lemon and lime

lemon and orange flower water

mango and grape

mango and lime

cherries and almond essence (extract)

apricots and almond essence (extract)

blackberry and mint

blackberry and apple

blackberry and rose water

melon and champagne

melon and strawberry

peach or nectarine and cinnamon

peach or nectarine and redcurrant

grapefruit and lemon or lime

infuse rose petals or mint leaves in the syrup as it cools (strain before freezing) and enliven the syrup with a measure of gin, vodka or bourbon.

◆ CIDER AND APPLE SORBET ◆ (SHERBET)

◇ INGREDIENTS ◇

SERVES 4

1 cup/225 ml/8 oz sugar
1¼ cups/300 ml/10 fl oz water
450 g/1 lb cooking apples
30 ml/2 tbsp water or apple juice
1¼ cups/300 ml/10 fl oz dry cider
30 ml/2 tbsp lemon or lime juice

◇ PREPARATION ◇

◇ Heat the sugar with the water over a medium heat, stirring until it has dissolved. Boil for 5 minutes and leave to cool.

◇ Peel, core and slice the apples. Cook over a low heat with the water or apple juice until tender. Cool and purée.

◇ Stir the cold apple purée into the syrup. Add the cider and lemon or lime juice. Mix well.

◇ Pour into a freezer tray or plastic box and freeze, stirring occasionally.

VARIATION For a cider sorbet (sherbet), omit the apples. Boil 2½ cups/575 ml/1 pt of cider with ½ cup/125 g/4 oz sugar for 5 minutes. Add 30 ml/2 tbsp of orange or lemon juice and freeze as above.

The cider can be spiced by adding a pinch of cinnamon, nutmeg and ground cloves.

A plain apple sorbet (sherbet) can be made in the same way — with or without spices — by replacing the cider with apple juice or sweet white wine.

PEAR AND GINGER SORBET (SHERBET)

◇ INGREDIENTS ◇

SERVES 4

¾ cup/175 g/6 oz sugar

2 cups/575 ml/16 fl oz water

1 lemon

3 medium pears

4 knobs stem ginger

◇ PREPARATION ◇

◇ Heat the sugar in the water over a medium heat, stirring until it has dissolved. Boil rapidly for 5 minutes.

◇ Grate the lemon rind and add to the syrup along with the juice of the lemon. Leave to cool.

◇ Peel the pears and remove the core. Mash or liquidize them to make a purée.

◇ Add the diced stem ginger and cold syrup. Mix well.

◇ Pour into a freezer tray or plastic box, cover and freeze. Stir regularly, mixing the ice crystals in well.

◆ MELON SORBET (SHERBET) ◆

◇ INGREDIENTS ◇

SERVES 4

¼ cup/50 g/2 oz sugar

1¼ cups/300 ml/10 fl oz water

2 cups/450 g/16 oz melon, puréed

30 ml/2 tbsp lemon or lime juice

◇ PREPARATION ◇

◇ Follow the instructions for pear and ginger sorbet (sherbet) (see page 87). Serve the sorbet (sherbet) in the melon shell and spoon a sauce of puréed mango, raspberry or peach over the top.
◇ Alternatively, add diced stem ginger or a pinch of ground ginger.

◆ FRESH MINT SORBET (SHERBET) ◆   SAVOURY SORBET (SHERBET) ◆

◇ I N G R E D I E N T S ◇
SERVES 4
¼ cup/50 g/2 oz sugar
1¼ cups/300 ml/10 fl oz water
6 large sprigs of fresh mint
1 lemon
1 egg white

◇ I N G R E D I E N T S ◇
SERVES 4
¼ cup/50 g/2 oz sugar
2½ cups/575 ml/1 pt water
30 ml/2 tbsp basil or marjoram leaves
1 lemon or lime
1 egg white

◇ P R E P A R A T I O N ◇

◇ Heat the sugar in the water over a medium heat, stirring until it has dissolved. Pour over the sprigs of mint and leave to infuse, like tea, for 20 minutes. Strain and mix with the juice of the lemon.

◇ Pour the syrup into a freezer tray or plastic box, cover and freeze for 2 hours. Whisk well.

◇ Whisk the egg white until it is stiff but not dry. Gently fold it into the half frozen syrup, starting with just one spoonful and gradually adding the remainder. Return to the freezer until frozen but still workable.

◇ P R E P A R A T I O N ◇

◇ Follow the instructions for fresh mint sorbet (sherbet).

VARIATION Replace the herbs with either a cinnamon stick, split vanilla pod or a few saffron threads.

◆ *FROZEN TOMATO CRUSH* ◆

◇ *I N G R E D I E N T S* ◇

SERVES 4
---
8 tomatoes
---
5 ml/1 tsp sugar
---
1 lemon
---
15 ml/1 tbsp fresh parsley, basil or marjoram

◇ *P R E P A R A T I O N* ◇

◇ Skin the tomatoes and liquidize. Combine the sugar, juice of the lemon and finely chopped herbs. Mix well with the tomato.

◇ Pour into a freezer tray or plastic box and freeze until firm, stirring occasionally. Scrape curls of the sorbet (sherbet) into a tall glass or transfer to the refrigerator for 45 minutes until it is slightly mushy then serve garnished with a sprig of parsley, basil or marjoram.

VARIATION For a spicy sorbet (sherbet), add a dash of Worcestershire or Tabasco sauce (hot pepper sauce).

◆ BLACK TEA SORBET (SHERBET) ◆

◇ I N G R E D I E N T S ◇

SERVES 4

¾ cup/175 g/6 oz sugar

2½ cups/450 ml/1 pt water

30 ml/2 tbsp China tea

2 limes

◇ P R E P A R A T I O N ◇

◇ Heat the sugar in the water over a medium heat, stirring until it has dissolved. Boil rapidly for 5 minutes. Pour over the tea leaves and infuse for 5 minutes. Strain.

◇ Grate the rind of the limes and stir into the hot tea along with the juice of both limes. Leave until cold.

◇ Pour into a freezer tray or plastic box, cover and freeze. Stir regularly, mixing the ice crystals around the edge into the centre.

VARIATION Vary the proportions of tea and lime juice, according to taste.

Vary the tea used — try Earl Grey, Darjeeling, Ceylon or herb or flower teas.

Substitute orange and/or lemon juice for the lime juice.

Add a measure of spirit to the syrup or pour it over the frozen sorbet (sherbet). Try rum, brandy or Curaçao.

Fold a whisked egg white into the partially frozen sorbet.

◆ MILK SHERBET ◆

◇ INGREDIENTS ◇

SERVES 4

3¾ cups/900 ml/1½ pt milk

¾ cup/175 g/6 oz sugar

1 orange

1 lemon

◇ PREPARATION ◇

◇ Mix the milk and sugar until the sugar is dissolved. Add the juice and finely grated rind of the orange or lemon. Stir well.

◇ Pour into a freezer tray or plastic box and freeze, stirring frequently, until the sherbet is firm.

VARIATIONS Use ¾ cup/175 ml/6 oz frozen concentrated orange juice, lemonade or mixed tropical fruit instead of the fresh fruit juice.

Substitute pineapple juice for orange juice.

The proportions of milk to fruit juice can be varied to taste.

Replace 1 cup/225 ml/8 fl oz milk with 1 cup/225 ml/8 fl oz single (light) cream.

Add a few drops of orange flower water to the sherbet.

Add a purée of soft fruit such as cranberries, blackberries, blackcurrants, raspberries to the sherbet before freezing.

Omit the fruit juice and add instant coffee or unsweetened cocoa to the sherbet instead.

◆ QUICK SORBET (SHERBET) ◆

◇ INGREDIENTS ◇

SERVES 4

1½ cups/350 ml/12 oz fruit purée

5 ml/1 tsp lemon juice

10 ml/2 tsp almond essence (extract) OR
30 ml/2 tbsp cherry brandy, Kirsch or apricot brandy

◇ PREPARATION ◇

◇ Use either fresh, poached or tinned (canned) fruit and mix the purée with the lemon juice and essence (extract) or liqueur. Pour into a freezer tray or plastic box and freeze, stirring occasionally, until nearly firm.

VARIATION Fold 2 stiffly beaten egg whites into the purée before freezing.

◆ QUICK FRUIT SORBET (SHERBET) ◆

◇ INGREDIENTS ◇

SERVES 4

½ cup/125 g/4 oz sugar

1¼ cups/300 ml/10 fl oz water

¾ cup/175 ml/6 fl oz frozen concentrated fruit juice

1 egg white

◇ PREPARATION ◇

◇ Heat the sugar with the water over a medium heat, stirring constantly until the sugar has dissolved. Boil rapidly for 5 minutes. Cool.
◇ Defrost the fruit juice until it is mushy. Stir in the syrup.
◇ Whisk the egg white until it is stiff but not dry. Carefully fold into the syrup, starting with one spoonful and gradually adding the remainder.
◇ Pour into a freezer tray or plastic box and freeze until nearly firm, stirring occasionally.

VARIATION Add 15 ml/1 tbsp of orange flower water to the sorbet (sherbet).
  Remove the seeds from 2 cardamom pods, crush lightly and stir into the syrup.

OPPOSITE: Quick Sorbet (Sherbet) (left) and Quick Fruit Sorbet (Sherbet) (right)

◆ WHITE WINE SORBET (SHERBET) ◆

◇ INGREDIENTS ◇

SERVES 8

¾ cup/175 g/6 oz sugar

⅔ cup/150 ml/5 fl oz water

2 oranges

2 lemons

2½ cups/575 ml/1 pt white wine

30 ml/2 tbsp brandy

2½ cups/575 ml/1 pt double (heavy) cream

◇ PREPARATION ◇

◇ Heat the sugar with the water over a medium heat until it has dissolved. Boil for 5 minutes. Add the juice of both the oranges and lemons. Leave to cool.

◇ Stir the wine and brandy into the cooled syrup.

◇ Whisk the cream until it is just beginning to thicken. Carefully fold into the wine and syrup.

◇ Pour into a freezer tray or plastic box and freeze, stirring frequently.

◇ Spoon or pipe into a wine glass while still slightly soft. A dash of wine or liqueur should be splashed on top.

VARIATIONS Use red wine, cider, Guinness or champagne instead of white wine. If you want a non-alcoholic sherbet, use grape juice, apple juice or lemonade.

Alter the proportions of orange and lemon juice to taste. Try substituting lime and/or grapefruit juice for all or part of the orange and lemon juice.

Replace the brandy with a liqueur of your choice.

Add a fruit purée to the wine mixture before adding the cream. Try redcurrants, peaches, apricots pineapple or mango.

Fold one or two stiffly beaten egg whites into the sherbet when it is half frozen. To make a Spoom sweeten the egg whites with ½ cup/125 g/4 oz sugar to make an Italian meringue.

◆ *FROZEN COCKTAIL SORBET (SHERBET)* ◆

◇ INGREDIENTS ◇

SERVES 4

1 lemon

10 ml/2 tsp sugar

dash Angostura bitters

½ cup/125 ml/4 fl oz whisky

1¼ cups/300 ml/10 fl oz double (heavy) cream

3 egg whites

◇ PREPARATION ◇

◇ Combine the lemon juice, sugar, bitters and whisky.

◇ Whisk the cream until it is just beginning to thicken. Stir into the whisky blend.

◇ Whisk the egg whites until they are stiff but not dry. Gently fold into the cocktail, starting with just one spoonful and gradually adding the remainder.

◇ Pour into a freezer tray or plastic box and freeze, stirring occasionally, until it is partly frozen. Spoon or pipe into a cocktail glass.

VARIATIONS Any cocktail can be made in the same way — try a frozen Martini, Daiquiri, Brandy Alexander, or Piña Colada. Simply mix the cocktail and add the cream and egg whites.

Omit the cream. Blend lemon, lime, orange or pineapple juice with a combination of liqueur and spirit. Freeze until it is partly frozen, fold in a whisked egg white and return to the freezer until not quite firm. Serve in the shell of the fruit or a cocktail glass and garnish with pieces of fruit.

◆ CRANBERRY YOGURT ICE ◆

◇ *I N G R E D I E N T S* ◇

SERVES 4

1½ cups/350 ml/12 fl oz cranberry sauce

1 orange or lemon

2 cups/450 ml/16 fl oz natural yogurt

◇ *P R E P A R A T I O N* ◇

◇ Combine the cranberry sauce with the finely grated rind and juice of the orange or lemon. Mix well.

◇ Lightly whisk the yogurt and gently fold into the cranberries.

◇ Turn into a freezer tray or plastic box and freeze, stirring occasionally.

VARIATIONS Substitute a sweetened blackcurrant or blackberry purée for the cranberry sauce. Sharpen with 15 ml/1 tbsp of lemon juice instead of the orange juice. Add a measure of Cassis if you have some.

◇ Any other type of fruit can be puréed and sweetened to taste and then mixed with yogurt and frozen as above. As with creamy yogurt ice cream (see page 31), the fruit can be flavoured with wine or liqueur and can be fresh or tinned (canned). You can also use dried fruit which has been poached in apple juice, water or wine.

Replace half or all of the yogurt with the same amount of whipping cream, whisked until it is just beginning to thicken.

Fold in one or two stiffly beaten egg whites either in addition to the yogurt and/or cream or instead of them.

◆ HONEY AND LEMON YOGURT ICE ◆

◇ *I N G R E D I E N T S* ◇

SERVES 4

½ cup/125 ml/4 oz honey

⅔ cup/150 ml/5 fl oz lemon juice

2 cups/450 ml/16 fl oz natural yogurt

◇ *P R E P A R A T I O N* ◇

◇ Dissolve the honey in the lemon juice. Proceed as for cranberry yogurt ice.

OPPOSITE: Cranberry Yogurt Ice (left) and Honey and Lemon Yogurt Ice (right)

Granitas

IF ICE was only available during the winter, but ices by their very nature were popular during the summer, how were they kept from melting? Early refrigerators were lined with zinc, and horse-drawn carts were seen on city streets delivering massive chunks for storage in chests. Ice picks were used to chip off manageable chunks as needed. Ice could then be combined with flavourings for sorbet or granita, or mixed with salt and used to pack metal containers holding cream to be frozen.

Earlier, wells were sunk or basements lined with straw to preserve the ice as long as possible. It was made and harvested during the winter, often by flooding fields and waiting for them to freeze. The resulting ice – and that from lakes and rivers – was cut into blocks and harvested. Many of the blocks were frozen so thoroughly that they were exported to warmer countries unable to manufacture sufficient quantities for themselves.

Today we can make ices and keep them thanks to the glories of refrigeration. Early fans of ices were forced by circumstance to eat them immediately and therefore had the pleasure of maximum flavour. Preserving ices detracts from their delicacy. The longer food is frozen, the more flavour it loses. So although we have the ability to keep sorbets and granitas stored in the freezer for some length of time, the question is, should we?

Early ices were made of fruit juice, honey or syrup poured over ice or snow. There was no added sugar, an ingredient which we may love but do not always need, at least not in the quantity which we now consume. The amount of sugar added to a sorbet or a granita is very important for another reason – it determines the consistency and can prevent the mixture freezing at all if too much is added.

Iced desserts became popular because they were light, refreshing and easily digestible. By using our freezers and ingredients advisedly, we can, and should, make sure that they stay that way.

◆ CHAMPAGNE GRANITA ◆

◇ INGREDIENTS ◇

SERVES 8

5 tbsp/65 g/2½ oz sugar

2 bottles champagne or sparkling wine

15 ml/1 tbsp lemon or lime juice

4 nectarines or peaches

8 sprigs mint leaves

◇ PREPARATION ◇

◇ Chill a shallow freezer proof dish for 1 hour.
◇ Sprinkle the sugar over the surface of the dish.
◇ Combine the lemon juice with one bottle of wine or champagne. Mix well.
◇ Pour into the dish. Freeze until nearly firm. Gently stir the ice crystals once or twice during freezing, but take care not to break them up.
◇ Place half a nectarine or peach in the bottom of a wine glass — slice the fruit if the glass is too narrow to hold it. Scrape the granita from the freezer dish and pile on top of the fruit. Fill the glass with champagne and garnish with mint leaves.

VARIATIONS Add a spoonful of finely chopped mint leaves to the champagne before freezing. Pour a measure of Crème de Menthe into the bottom of each glass before adding the granita and champagne.

Use any sweet white wine instead of champagne.

Vary the fruit used. Strawberries and oranges go particularly well with champagne.

Pour 15 ml/1 tbsp liqueur into the bottom of the wine glass before adding the granita and champagne or wine. Vary the taste according to the fruit used.

Serve the granita with fruit and liqueur if you want to use it, but don't fill the glass with the additional champagne or wine.

Any other fresh fruit granita such as strawberry or cherry can be served in the same way. For a non-alcoholic granita, fill the glass with orange juice, lemonade, soda water or sparkling mineral water.

◆ CLARET GRANITA ◆

◇ INGREDIENTS ◇

SERVES 4

¾ cup/175 g/6 oz sugar

¾ cup/175 g/6 fl oz water

1 orange

1 lemon or lime

1 bottle red wine

◇ PREPARATION ◇

◇ Heat the sugar with the water over a medium heat, stirring constantly until the sugar has dissolved. Boil for 1 minute.

◇ Add the juice of the orange and lemon or lime and leave the syrup to cool. Stir the wine into the syrup.

◇ Pour the granita mixture into a very shallow freezer proof dish and freeze until nearly firm. Stir the ice crystals at the edge of the dish into the centre several times but take care not to break them up — the granita should be fairly coarse.

◇ Pile the granita into goblets and serve garnished with fresh fruit — perhaps a slice of lemon or a few blackberries, or a sprig of mint or lemon balm.

VARIATIONS Substitute cider for claret.

Substitute apple, pineapple or grape juice for claret.

Serve as for champagne granita (see page 102), piling it into a tall glass or goblet and filling the glass with wine, mineral water or orange juice.

◆ COFFEE GRANITA ◆

◇ INGREDIENTS ◇

SERVES 4

½ cup/125 g/4 oz sugar

¾ cup/175 ml/6 fl oz water

2 cups/450 ml/16 fl oz strong black coffee or espresso

◇ PREPARATION ◇

◇ Heat the sugar with the water over a medium heat, stirring constantly until the sugar has dissolved. Boil for 5 minutes. Leave to cool.

◇ Stir the syrup into the cold coffee or espresso.

◇ Pour the granita mixture into a very shallow freezer proof dish and freeze until nearly firm. Stir the ice crystals at the edge of the dish into the centre several times but take care not to break them up — the granita should be fairly coarse.

◇ Scrape the granita crystals from the dish and pile into tall glasses or sundae coupes. Serve topped with whipped cream and a sprinkling of grated chocolate.

VARIATION Infuse a cinnamon stick, a strip of orange rind or a few cloves in the syrup while it is cooling. Strain before using.

Stir a measure of coffee liqueur, brandy or orange or chocolate liqueur into the syrup along with the coffee.

Add ¼ cup/50 g/2 oz melted unsweetened chocolate to the coffee.

Omit the sugar syrup. Combine finely ground coffee with sugar to taste and infuse in boiling water for 30 minutes. Strain, cool and freeze as above.

◆ STRAWBERRY GRANITA ◆

◇ INGREDIENTS ◇

SERVES 4

½ *cup/125 g/4 oz sugar*
¾ *cup/175 ml/6 fl oz water*
2⅔ *cups/450 g/1 lb fresh strawberries*
15 *ml/1 tbsp lemon juice*

◇ PREPARATION ◇

◇ Heat the sugar with the water over a medium heat, stirring constantly until it has dissolved. Boil for 5 minutes. Leave to cool.

◇ Purée the strawberries and sieve to remove any seeds. Mix in the lemon juice.

◇ Stir the syrup into the strawberry purée.

◇ Pour the granita mixture into a very shallow freezer proof dish and freeze until nearly firm. Stir the ice crystals at the edge of the dish into the centre several times but take care not to break them up — the granita should be fairly coarse.

VARIATIONS Flavour the granita with Grand Marnier, orange flower water or the juice of 1 orange.

Omit the sugar syrup. Purée and sieve the strawberries. Sweeten with icing (confectioners') sugar, add orange and/or lemon juice to taste and freeze.

Mix half frozen granita with partially defrosted concentrated orange juice.

Use half strawberries and half raspberries.

Frozen fruit can be used instead of fresh fruit but use half the amount of sugar.

◆ ORANGE GRANITA ◆

◇ I N G R E D I E N T S ◇
SERVES 4

¾ cup/175 g/6 oz sugar

2 cups/450 ml/16 fl oz water

1 lemon

2–3 oranges

15 ml/1 tbsp orange flower water (optional)

◇ P R E P A R A T I O N ◇

◇ Heat the sugar in the water over a medium heat, stirring constantly until the sugar has dissolved. Boil for 5 minutes.

◇ Add the finely grated peel of the lemon and both oranges to the syrup. Leave until completely cold.

◇ Stir the juice of the lemon and oranges into the syrup. Add the orange flower water if you are using it.

◇ Pour the granita mixture into a very shallow freezer proof dish and freeze until nearly firm. Stir the ice crystals at the edge of the dish into the centre several times but take care not to break them up — the granita should be fairly coarse.

VARIATIONS Use tangerines instead of oranges.

Do not use the peel of the oranges. Squeeze the juice from the fruit carefully, keeping the shells intact, and spoon the frozen granita back into the shells for serving.

◆ TEA GRANITA ◆

◇ I N G R E D I E N T S ◇
SERVES 4

30 ml/2 tbsp tea leaves (Orange Pekoe, Darjeeling, Ceylon, rosehip or any other kind)

45 ml/3 tbsp sugar

30 ml/2 tbsp lemon or lime juice

2½ cups/575 ml/1 pt boiling water

◇ P R E P A R A T I O N ◇

◇ Combine the tea leaves, sugar and juice. Pour over the boiling water, mix well and leave until cold. Strain and freeze as for coffee granita (see page 104).

VARIATION Infuse mint leaves or lemon balm in the tea while it is cooling. Strain before freezing. Pour a measure of Crème de Menthe over the granita before serving.

◆ CHOCOLATE GRANITA ◆

◇ I N G R E D I E N T S ◇
SERVES 4

¾ cup/75 g/3 oz unsweetened cocoa

45 ml/3 tbsp sugar

2½ cups/575 ml/1 pt boiling water

◇ P R E P A R A T I O N ◇

◇ Combine the cocoa and sugar. Pour over the boiling water, mix well and leave until cold. Freeze as for coffee granita (see page 104).

OPPOSITE: Orange Granita
(*see* above)

◆ *LEMON GRANITA* ◆ *HONEY AND LEMON GRANITA* ◆

◇ *INGREDIENTS* ◇
SERVES 4
¾ cup/175 g/6 oz sugar
2 cups/450 ml/16 fl oz water
¾ cup/175 ml/6 fl oz lemon juice
15 ml/1 tbsp orange flower water (optional)

◇ *INGREDIENTS* ◇
SERVES 4
2 lemons
2½ cups/575 ml/1 pt boiling water
¼ cup/50 ml/2 oz honey

◇ *PREPARATION* ◇

◇ As for orange granita (see page 107).

VARIATION Substitute lime juice for lemon juice.

◇ *PREPARATION* ◇

◇ Infuse the lemon rinds in boiling water for 10 minutes. Add the honey and stir until dissolved. Add the juice of the lemons, mix well and cool completely.
◇ Strain the granita mixture, pour into a very shallow freezer proof dish and freeze as for orange granita (see page 107).

VARIATIONS Serve the granita with a measure of whisky or rum poured over it.

Serve the granita in a dish or melon shell mixed with blackberries, melon balls or sliced mango.

◆ *ALTERNATIVE FRUIT* ◆ *GRANITAS*

◇ Purée and sieve raspberries or blackberries. Proceed as for strawberry granita (see page 105).

◇ Purée melon or pineapple. Proceed as for strawberry granita.

◇ Poach grapes, plums, cherries, peaches, pears, apricots or nectarines in sugar syrup until soft. Remove the stones (pits) and sieve to make a smooth purée. Proceed as for strawberry granita.

◇ Cook red, white or blackcurrants with sugar over a very low heat until the juices run free. Sieve and liquidize. Proceed as for strawberry granita.

◇ Infuse a cinnamon stick, split vanilla pod, bruised mint leaves or orange, lemon or lime peel in the syrup while it cools.

◇ Flavour any of the fruit purées with a complimentary liqueur or spirit.

◇ Serve any of these fruit granitas as for champagne granita (see page 102).

Biscuits (Cookies), Sauces and Decorations

AND SO to the crowning glory – those ingredients which enhance, garnish and decorate, which can complement or contrast and turn an ice into a masterpiece. Is there anything that does not go with ice cream? Is there any time of day or night when it cannot be served? Is there any occasion that cannot be better celebrated with ice cream than without it?

The recipes given earlier often include serving suggestions and recommendations for variations or accompaniments. The recipes that follow detail some of them. Nearly every cookbook includes a section on desserts, full of ideas for cakes, biscuits (cookies), sweets (candies) and sauces that can be served with ice cream.

The aim of this book is to inspire a sense of fun. We have laid the groundwork. You can follow any or all of the recipes, work your way through your first page to last, but homemade ice cream is first and foremost for pleasure. The more imagination you put into creating your iced desserts, the more you will enjoy the finished product. Enjoyment is what ice cream is all about.

◆ LANGUES DE CHAT ◆

◇ I N G R E D I E N T S ◇

7 tbsp/90 g/3½ oz unsalted (sweet) butter

½ cup/125 g/4 oz sugar

3 egg whites

1 tsp/5 ml vanilla essence (extract)

2 tbsp/30 ml single (light) cream

1 cup/125 g/4 oz flour

oven: 220°C/425°F/Gas 7

◇ P R E P A R A T I O N ◇

◇ Cream the butter and sugar until very light and fluffy.

◇ Lightly whisk the egg whites. Stir into the butter mixture along with the vanilla and cream.

◇ Gently fold in the sieved (sifted) flour.

◇ Spoon or pipe the batter onto a well greased tray (cookie sheet), allowing enough space for the biscuits (cookies) to spread while they are baking. Langues de Chat are traditionally finger shaped, but if you are planning to make baskets (see below), spread the mixture into 10 cm/4 in circles.

◇ Bake in a preheated oven for 5 minutes.

◇ Leave the biscuits (cookies) to cool on the tray for a few minutes before transferring to a wire rack.

VARIATION When the langues de chat have cooled, their ends can be dipped into melted chocolate. Place the biscuits (cookies) on a sheet of greaseproof (waxed) paper for the chocolate to set.

To make baskets (*tulipes*) which can be filled with scoops of sorbet (sherbet) or ice cream, quickly lift the hot, soft biscuits (cookies) with a spatula and gently press over upturned cups or moulds (molds) or slightly greased oranges. Leave to cool.

◇ Baskets or *tulipes* can be made from batter flavoured with almond paste, orange or lemon rind or the mixture usually used for brandy snaps. Be sure to work quickly and shape the freshly baked biscuits (cookies) before they have time to cool and firm.

◆ *TRUFFLES* ◆

◇ *I N G R E D I E N T S* ◇

MAKES 12

½ cup/50 g/2 oz icing (confectioners') sugar

¼ cup/50 g/2 oz unsalted (sweet) butter

¾ cup/75 g/3 oz ground almonds

2½ ml/½ tsp almond essence (extract) or 5 ml/1 tsp rum

15 ml/3 tsp unsweetened cocoa

1½ cups/75 g/3 oz cake crumbs

45 ml/3 tbsp chocolate strands

◇ *P R E P A R A T I O N* ◇

◇ Beat the sugar with the butter until light and smooth. Add all remaining ingredients except the chocolate strands. Mix well. Roll the mixture into 12 small balls and coat each with chocolate strands.

◇ The truffles can also be rolled in finely chopped almonds or glacé (candied) cherries if you prefer.

VARIATION

⅓ cup/75 g/3 oz plain (dark) chocolate pieces

15 ml/1 tbsp unsalted butter

1 egg yolk

5 ml/1 tsp rum

5 ml/1 tsp single (light) cream

¼ cup/25 g/1 oz cocoa powder

1½ cups/75 g/3 oz cake crumbs

¾ cup/75 g/3 oz ground almonds

45 ml/3 tbsp chocolate strands

◇ Break the chocolate and melt in the top of a double boiler. Add all the remaining ingredients except the chocolate strands. Proceed as above.

◆ SWISS MERINGUE ◆

◇ INGREDIENTS ◇

2 egg whites

½ cup/125 g/4 oz caster (fine) sugar

oven: 120°C/250°F/Gas ½

◇ PREPARATION ◇

◇ Whisk the egg whites until they are stiff enough to make peaks when you lift the whisk out. Gently fold in the sugar, a little bit at a time, and whisk until the meringue is glossy and thick enough to hold its shape.

◇ Spoon or pipe the meringue onto greased baking sheets lined with silicone paper or vegetable parchment. Individual meringues can be sandwiched together with ice cream or larger meringue layers used to make a gâteau with ice cream between the layers. Meringue baskets can be filled with fruit and ice cream and topped with chantilly cream.

◇ Miniature meringues can also be used to decorate sundaes. Pipe the unbaked meringue into rosettes, fingers, rings or any other shape. Fill them with ice cream or use them as a garnish. Another alternative is to pipe the meringue into individual cupcake tins, leaving a hollow centre which will later be filled with ice cream or sorbet.

◇ Bake in a preheated oven for 1 hour. If the meringues are not completely dried out, continue baking for 30 minutes longer.

VARIATION Gently fold unsweetened cocoa, instant coffee or ground nuts into the meringue before baking.

◆ CHANTILLY CREAM ◆

◇ INGREDIENTS ◇

1¼ cups/300 ml/10 fl oz double (heavy) cream

15 ml/1 tbsp caster (fine) sugar

5 ml/1 tsp vanilla essence (extract)

◇ PREPARATION ◇

◇ Whisk the cream until it is just beginning to thicken. Add the sugar and vanilla essence (extract) and continue whisking until the cream is stiff enough to hold its shape.

OPPOSITE: Swiss Meringue
(*see* above)

◆ *ITALIAN MERINGUE* ◆

◇ INGREDIENTS ◇

½ cup/125 g/4 oz caster (fine) sugar

⅓ cup/65 ml/2½ fl oz water

2 egg whites

oven: 120°C/250°F/Gas ½

◇ PREPARATION ◇

◇ Stir the sugar in the water over a medium heat until it has dissolved. Boil for 5 minutes.

◇ Whisk the egg whites until they are stiff but not dry.

◇ Slowly pour the hot syrup over the egg whites, whisking constantly, until the meringue is thick and has cooled completely.

◇ Spoon or pipe the meringue onto greased baking sheets lined with silicone paper (waxed paper) or vegetable parchment.

◇ Alternatively, use to seal the rings and decorate the outside of a vacherin Italian meringue can be used in any of the ways mentioned for Swiss meringue. The mixture is somewhat easier to make, goes further because the syrup makes it expand, and produces a slightly softer meringue.

◇ Bake in a preheated oven for 1 hour. If the meringues are not completely dried out, continue baking for 30 minutes longer.

VARIATION Gently fold unsweetened cocoa, instant coffee or ground nuts into the meringue before baking.

Italian Meringue can also be mixed with whipped cream or pastry cream and served as a topping/filling for baked meringues or cream puffs.

◆ *PRALINE* ◆

◇ I N G R E D I E N T S ◇

MAKES ¾ CUP/125 G/4 OZ

½ *cup/125 g/4 oz sugar*

½ *cup/125 g/4 oz blanched almonds*

a little oil

◇ P R E P A R A T I O N ◇

◇ Put the sugar and nuts in the bottom of a heavy based pan. Cook on a very low heat, stirring constantly, until the sugar has melted and turned a golden brown colour. Be sure that all the nuts are well coated.

◇ Brush a flat baking tray (cookie sheet) with oil.

Spread the nuts and syrup onto the tray and leave until set.

◇ Crush the praline with a rolling pin or food processor. It can be coarse or fine, according to personal preference. Alternatively, simply break it into uneven slabs. Use the praline as a garnish, or flavour ice cream with ground praline. Chunks of praline can also be stirred into a softened ice cream or bombe to provide a contrast in texture.

VARIATION Use peanuts, hazelnuts (filberts), walnuts or pecans instead of almonds.

GLAZED NUTS: Melt the sugar as above and dip the nuts in one at a time. Remove and leave to cool on a sheet of greaseproof (waxed) paper.

◆ *GLAZED FRUIT* ◆

◇ *I N G R E D I E N T S* ◇

1 cup/225 g/8 oz sugar

30 ml/2 tbsp water

strawberries, grapes, cherries, pineapple, etc.

◇ *P R E P A R A T I O N* ◇

◇ Heat the sugar with the water over a low flame, stirring constantly, until the sugar has dissolved. Boil rapidly for 5 minutes.

◇ Wash the pieces of fruit and leave to dry. Leave the occasional stem or leaf attached. Dip the fruit into the hot syrup and cool on a wire rack. Any available fruit can be glazed in this way.

VARIATION FOR FROSTED FRUIT whisk an egg white until it is frothy. Dip the fruit into the egg white then coat with sugar. Dry on a wire rack. Tiny flowers or leaves can be frosted in the same way.

For CHOCOLATE FRUIT, see page 120.

◆ *BRANDIED FRUIT* ◆

◇ *I N G R E D I E N T S* ◇

2 cups/450 g/1 lb sugar

3 cups/675 ml/1¼ pt water

peaches, plums, cherries, mandarin or tangerine oranges

1 cup/225 ml/8 fl oz brandy (approx.)

◇ *P R E P A R A T I O N* ◇

◇ Stir the sugar in the water on a low heat until it has dissolved.

◇ Plunge peaches, plums or any other firm fruit which needs peeling into boiling water for 1 minute. Remove and skin. Poach the fruit in the syrup until it is tender. Prick with a skewer or fork.

◇ If the fruit does not need to be cooked (for example cherries, mandarin or tangerine oranges) simply pierce with a skewer or fork. If you prefer, cut it into cubes or slices.

◇ Pack the fruit into jars. Pour some brandy into each jar (the amount depends on personal prefer-ence) top up with syrup and seal well.

◇ Store the fruit for at least one month before using.

◇ Strain the alcohol off to serve as a drink and spoon the fruit over ice cream or use as the centre of a bombe. The fruit can also be puréed with a small amount of alcohol to make a sauce — serve hot or cold. Alternatively, drizzle the fruit liqueur over one or more scoops of ice cream or sorbet.

VARIATIONS Substitute gin or rum for the brandy.

For a mixed fruit jar, find a large stone crock and start off with 2 cups/450 ml/16 fl oz of brandy. Add fruit as it comes into season, using any combination, according to personal taste. For each 450 g/1 lb of fruit, add the same amount of sugar. Cover well, stir daily and keep for at least one month, to allow the alcohol and sugar to penetrate the fruit thoroughly.

Preserve various fruits with the corresponding liqueur. For example, oranges in Armagnac or Curaçao, cherries or pineapple in Kirsch, mango in Bols, or plums in gin.

◆ CHOCOLATE DECORATIONS ◆

◇ Break as much chocolate as you think you'll need into a bowl which just fits over a pan. Fill the pan with water to come just under the bottom of the bowl. Bring the water to the boil, remove from the heat and place the bowl in the pan. Stir the chocolate until it has melted.

◇ Spread the chocolate on a baking (cookie) sheet and leave to set. Use a sharp knife or metal spatula to scrape the chocolate off the sheet into curls.

◇ Alternatively, line the baking sheet with greaseproof (waxed) paper. When the chocolate has cooled, turn onto a sheet of clean paper, remove the lining paper and cut into squares, diamonds or other shapes with either a sharp knife or an aspic cutter.

CHOCOLATE CUPS: Spoon the chocolate mixture into moulds (molds) and immediately empty the chocolate out again. If you want the cups to be very thick, wait until one layer of chocolate has set and then repeat the process until the cup is the desired thickness. When the chocolate has cooled, loosen the edges with a sharp knife and remove the mould (mold).

CHOCOLATE LEAVES: Dip one side of a leaf (for example, a rose or bay leaf) in the chocolate mixture and leave to dry on a wire rack or a sheet of greaseproof (waxed) paper. When the chocolate has set, carefully peel off the leaf.

CHOCOLATE FRUIT: Dip pieces of fruit into the melted chocolate and set to dry on a wire rack.

HOME-MADE JELLY (JELLO)

◇ INGREDIENTS ◇

1 tbsp/15 g/½ oz powdered or 6 leaves gelatine (gelatin)
½ cup/125 g/4 oz sugar
2 cups/450 ml/16 fl oz water
1½ cups/350 g/12 oz fruit OR
⅔ cup/150 ml/5 fl oz orange juice
45 ml/3 tbsp lemon juice

◇ PREPARATION ◇

◇ If you are using gelatine (gelatin) leaves, soften them in a little bit of water.

◇ Heat and stir the sugar into the water.

◇ Remove from the heat, add the gelatine (gelatin) and stir until it has dissolved.

◇ Purée the fruit and sieve (strain). Use soft fruit.

◇ Add the gelatine (gelatin) to the fruit purée or orange juice. Stir in the lemon juice and cool.

◇ Pour the jelly (jello) into a mould (mold), an attractive serving dish or several glasses and chill to set. Set the jelly in a ring mould (mold) and fill the centre with scoops of ice cream and/or sorbet (sherbet) or set in an ordinary bowl and then chop the jelly (jello) when it is firm. Arrange on a serving dish or spoon into several glasses. Place scoops of ice cream or sorbet (sherbet) on top.

VARIATIONS Any fruit juice you like can be substituted for the orange juice. Adjust the quantity of sugar to taste. More juice and less water can be used for a stronger flavour.

Flavour the jelly with wine, champagne, port or liqueur or soak the fruit you are using in wine or liqueur.

Flavour milk with chocolate, coffee or fruit syrup or milkshake powder. Heat, dissolve gelatine (gelatin) and cool until thick. Refrigerate until firm.

Pour half of the jelly into a mould (mold) or dish and refrigerate until nearly firm. Top with a layer of fruit and pour over the remaining jelly.

Use several flavours, with or without fruit between the layers. Always let the bottom layer set before adding the next layer.

◆ *FRUIT SAUCE* ◆

Cranberry Crush   Fruit Sauce   Citrus Sauce

◇ I N G R E D I E N T S ◇

MAKES 1 CUP/225 ML/8 FL OZ

1–1½ cups/225 g/8 oz fresh, tinned (canned) or frozen fruit

¼ cup/50 ml/2 fl oz red or white wine

5 ml/1 tsp almond essence (extract) or 5 ml/1 tsp lemon juice

◇ P R E P A R A T I O N ◇

◇ Simmer the fruit in the wine until it is soft. Sieve or purée it and add the almond essence (extract) or sharpen with lemon juice.

◇ Any fruit at all can be used for this sauce and a combination of two or more fruits create exciting tastes.

VARIATIONS Rather than flavouring the fruit with almond essence (extract), add a cinnamon stick or split vanilla pod to the fruit while it is cooking. Remove before puréeing the fruit, but add a pinch of ground cinnamon or the seeds of the vanilla pod to the finished sauce.

Soft fruit such as strawberries, raspberries or blackcurrants can be cooked without liquid — simply sprinkle with sugar and heat very gently until the fruit is soft.

Alternatively, liquidize or purée the fruit first, boil until it thickens slightly and flavour with wine and vanilla essence (extract). For a non-alcoholic sauce, omit the wine. For a more alcoholic sauce, use spirit or liqueur.

A knob of butter can also be stirred into the hot fruit purée.

◆ CITRUS SAUCE ◆

◇ INGREDIENTS ◇

MAKES 1 CUP/225 ML/8 FL OZ

2 lemons or limes OR 1 orange

45 ml/3 tbsp sugar

15 ml/1 tbsp arrowroot

1 cup/225 ml/8 fl oz water

◇ PREPARATION ◇

◇ Finely grate the rind of the lemons, lime or orange.

◇ Combine the sugar and arrowroot. Slowly add the fruit juice. Stir in the water and grated rind. Cook the sauce over a low heat, stirring constantly, until it begins to thicken and turns clear.

◇ For a thinner sauce, omit the arrowroot. Combine all the ingredients and stir over a low heat until the sugar dissolves.

VARIATION Use poached or tinned (canned) fruit, thicken the liquid as above and gently stir in the fruit for a minute or two to heat through.

◆ CRANBERRY CRUSH ◆

◇ INGREDIENTS ◇

MAKES 1 CUP/225 ML/8 FL OZ

1 cup/225 ml/8 oz cranberry sauce

30 ml/2 tbsp gin or vodka

◇ PREPARATION ◇

◇ Heat the cranberry sauce gently with the gin or vodka until well mixed.

◇ Any other fruit preserve, jam or marmalade can be turned into a sauce in the same way with the addition of white wine, liqueur or lemon juice. A strip of lemon or orange peel can also be heated with the sauce.

CHOCOLATE SAUCE

◇ INGREDIENTS ◇

¼ cup/50 g/2 oz plain (dark) chocolate

½ cup/125 g/4 oz brown sugar

⅓ cup/65 g/2½ fl oz double (heavy) cream

10 ml/2 tsp grated orange rind (optional) OR
5 ml/1 tsp mint flavouring or almond essence (extract)

30 ml/2 tbsp Cointreau, Kirsch or rum

◇ PREPARATION ◇

◇ Break the chocolate into the top of a double boiler. Add the sugar and cream. Heat, stirring occasionally, until the chocolate has melted and the sauce is smooth.
◇ Stir in the orange rind, flavouring and liqueur. Mix well.

VARIATIONS Add strong black coffee or a pinch of ground ginger or cinnamon to the sauce.

Two spoonfuls of crunchy peanut butter, or a few finely chopped marshmallows, nuts or cherries can also be stirred in.

QUICK CHOCOLATE SAUCE: Simply melt 1 cup/225 ml/8 oz of chocolate, broken into pieces, in the top of a double boiler and mix with enough whipped cream to make a smooth sauce. Flavour as above. Alternatively, melt the chocolate and stir in 4 tbsp/50 g/2 oz unsalted (sweet) butter. Beat until smooth.

COFFEE SAUCE

◇ INGREDIENTS ◇

MAKES 1 CUP/225 ML/8 FL OZ

½ cup/125 g/4 oz demerara sugar

30 ml/2 tbsp water

1¼ cups/300 ml/10 fl oz black coffee

◇ PREPARATION ◇

◇ Stir the sugar in the water over a low heat until it has dissolved. Boil until the syrup is a light golden colour. Add the coffee and boil until it thickens slightly and turns syrupy.

VARIATION Kahlua, Tia Maria, Drambuie or Crème de Cacao can be added to this sauce.

MAPLE SAUCE

◇ INGREDIENTS ◇

MAKES 1 CUP/225 ML/8 FL OZ

1 cup/225 ml/8 fl oz maple syrup

½ cup/125 ml/4 fl oz whipping cream

◇ PREPARATION ◇

◇ Boil the syrup until it thickens slightly.
◇ Whisk the cream until it is thick. Carefully fold in the syrup.

VARIATIONS Chopped walnuts or pecans can be mixed into the syrup; the syrup can be made up from a blend of maple and honey.

◆ BUTTERSCOTCH SAUCE ◆

◇ INGREDIENTS ◇
MAKES ½ CUP/125 ML/4 FL OZ

¼ cup/50 g/2 oz brown sugar

30 ml/2 tbsp white sugar

15 ml/1 tbsp golden (light corn) syrup

⅓ cup/65 ml/2½ fl oz double (heavy) cream

10 ml/2 tsp unsalted (sweet) butter

few drops vanilla essence (extract)

◇ PREPARATION ◇
◇ Heat all the ingredients except the vanilla essence (extract) until the sugars have dissolved and the sauce is smooth. Stir in the vanilla essence (extract).

◆ MARSHMALLOW SAUCE ◆

◇ INGREDIENTS ◇
MAKES 1 CUP/225 ML/8 FL OZ

1 cup/125 g/4 oz small marshmallows

1 cup/125 g/4 oz icing (confectioners') sugar

60 ml/4 tbsp boiling water

◇ PREPARATION ◇
◇ Melt the marshmallows in the top of a double boiler. Mix until smooth.
◇ Add the sieved (sifted) sugar and the water. Mix well.

◆ RUM SAUCE ◆

◇ INGREDIENTS ◇
MAKES 1 CUP/225 ML/8 FL OZ

1 egg yolk

¼ cup/25 g/1 oz unsweetened cocoa

¼ cup/25 g/1 oz icing (confectioners') sugar

45 ml/3 tbsp rum

½ cup/125 ml/4 fl oz whipping cream

◇ PREPARATION ◇
◇ Beat the egg yolk with the cocoa and sugar until well blended.
◇ Add the rum and whisk until light and fluffy.
◇ Whisk the cream until it is thick. Gently fold into the rum mixture.
◇ Chill before serving.
◇ For a hot rum sauce, dissolve sugar in melted butter and stir in rum, ground cinnamon and orange juice to taste.

INDEX